How to Handle Your Human Relations

Lois Haines Sargent

ISBN: 0-86690-153-1

Current Printing: 1997

Published by:
American Federation of Astrologers, Inc.
PO Box 22040
6535 S. Rural Road
Tempe, AZ 85285-2040

Printed in the United States of America

Contents

Part 1

Part II

Part One

Chapter 1
Human Relationships

The ability to get along harmoniously with our fellow men is an asset impossible to overestimate. The success and happiness of every individual rests upon it. There is scarcely any activity or situation of life that does not involve contact with other human beings. The more easily a person adjusts himself to the family, community, and the associations he forms in earning his livelihood, the smoother will be his path in life. Nearly all the tension and strain of modern living is brought about, not by difficult conditions, but by disturbing emotions aroused in personal, group, or public contacts.

Civilization puts human personality to many tests. The closer the proximity people have to each other, the more readily will any faults or weaknesses of personality reveal themselves. Close relationships test the soul and character of individuals, but in such testings, character is developed and refined. The maturing person will learn something from every human encounter in which a feeling of resistance is aroused.

Psychology, which at one time advocated complete freedom of expression as the way to success and happiness, now recognizes the fact that individualism can be carried to an extreme. When it is, we find an egocentric, selfish, irresponsible, or undisciplined personality who makes life difficult for himself and others. He may even become antisocial or lawless. On the other extreme, to suppress individuality completely to ensure tranquil relationships can frustrate the normal unfolding of personality and talent. Such repressions can produce inner resentments which threaten the health, happiness, and worldly progress of the individual. Neither the completely self-centered, nor the completely self-effacing individual can fulfill himself and find the satisfaction in living that all humans seek.

A well-integrated personality achieves the happy balance between selfish individualism and supine compliance to the will of others. He will develop self-reliance, independence of thought, initiative and self-confidence while also recognizing the interdependence of people in a society. He will respect the rights of others. Every individual is dependent upon other individuals to some extent. This dependence does not mean leaning upon them. It is part of the give and take of life. Education, government, business, recreation, sports, entertainment, social life, research, trade, buying and selling, distribution, or anything else you can name, will make use of this interdependence of human beings. No one can deny it; to ignore it is not only foolish, but fatal to happiness and achievement. We may therefore accept the fact that one of the tasks of life, as Alfred Adler has termed the fundamental human problems, is that of learning how to live with our fellow men.

The first requisite is an understanding of human nature itself, irrespective of individual types and temperaments. There is a similarity in all human beings, because we all have similar desires, instincts, urges, and emotions. We know this, but do not always take it into consideration in our relationships.

An ambitious man in a large corporation works hard to advance himself, aiming for a certain promotion. Should another show the same ambition, it may be resented by the first man. Yet both are responding to a desire for importance or power (or more money) inherent in their natures. Recognizing rivalry, a well-balanced personality will view it as a challenge to make greater effort. He will do his best and let the best man win. The man who lacks self-confidence will become jealous of the rival, may become antagonistic in his attitude to him, and may even try to undermine him. In the long run the jealous individual defeats himself by his conduct.

The second requisite for getting along with others is self-understanding and self-control. If you understand yourself, you will find it easier to understand others. Self-control enables you to handle your contacts adroitly.

Astrologers believe that understanding of other individuals can be greatly simplified if you happen to know their birthdays. The general temperament of an individual is revealed in the birth sign. Even if one cannot obtain the complete birth data to erect a horoscope, he will understand much if he knows the birthday, which tells in what sign the person was born. Such understanding can or should give charity of judgment if nothing more.

Astrology emphasizes **self-understanding** because you must know where your own faults lie in adjusting yourself to others. In a horoscope we read individual personality through the sign ascending at the hour of birth; therefore the opposite point (seventh house) is one's projected attitude toward others, or what we call the general public. But every square or opposition aspect in the horoscope can be viewed as a personality trait which tests one's ability to get along harmoniously with others. The testing may not crop out as an open conflict, and the more emotionally mature the individual is, the less apt it is to do so. In this case it remains a psychological factor, part of the character or spiritual growth. Such a tension or problem of adjustment may present itself in family relationships or marriage, or in business or friendships. The planets symbolize one's instincts and urges, and if there is an inner conflict, as indicated by a square or opposition in the individual horoscope, and by some of the conjunctions (principally those in which one of the malefics is involved), this inner conflict will express itself in many, though probably not all, of its human contacts.

Bear in mind that in comparing horoscopes you are analyzing the effect of **one individual upon another.** In applying the rules for making comparisons do not overlook this fact. The purpose of comparing horoscopes is to explore the possibilities and problems of an association; to understand why another person affects you as he does and how you are apt to affect him.

It is a law of attraction as true in metaphysics as in psychology and astrology that our attracting or being attracted to certain persons or environments is rarely, if ever, pure chance.

When the association, or environment is testing or unpleasant, the experience has been attracted because of a conflict of personality in the individual nature that needs to be resolved. We must come to terms with our own conflicting urges. Sometimes the test may be to our discrimination in accepting or refusing a situation or an association. Some individuals may need to develop courage and will power to say "no" to an association that could be harmful to them.

For example: A person who is inclined to self-indulgence and knows himself to be weak in this respect should have courage to refuse friendship with another individual who is equally weak and so inclined to encourage him in his own weakness. A person who inclines to be timid may unconsciously choose as a marriage partner one who is aggressive and domineering, thereby prolonging his tendency to lean on others. Anyone overdeveloped in some aspect of his personality is apt to attract, as a mate, one who is underdeveloped in that particular trait, as long as he is unaware of his one-sidedness or is unable to balance it.

When the individual knows himself he will realize wherein his personality needs strengthening, improving, and disciplining, and thus he will know when to refuse an association, just as he will understand what he must learn from the relationships he cannot or will not sever.

Suggested Reading

Why We Behave Like Human Beings, George A Dorsey, Harper Bros.
Understanding Human Nature, Alfred Adler, Garden City Publishing Co.

Chapter 2
Love And Marriage

Men and women marry for many reasons; for a home, money, or security, but usually because they think they are in love - at least, in the United States. At times a person imagines himself in love with someone who can supply a lack. Regardless of any hidden psychological motivation for marriage, most couples marry because they feel for each other an emotion which at the time they describe as love.

Now, it is presumed that every mature person recognizes the fact that love and marriage are not synonymous. Romantic youth often make this mistake, expecting marriage to be a continuous courtship. Nor does all the scientific information available to us today serve to eradicate completely this ideal. It was probably this that inspired the cynical comment that "love is blind but marriage is an eye-opener."

The misogamist Schopenhauer somewhere wrote that love was a deception practiced by nature. It is quite true that what many young people (and older ones too for that matter) mistake for love is simply the biological urge glamorized. This is why marriage counselors advise couples to know each other at least six months before marrying. A year or two is even better.

It takes time for the first flush of infatuation to wear off so that two individuals can discover whether there are sufficient mutual interests and viewpoints, and enough harmony of disposition and personality to ensure compatibility, and that there are no serious conflicts of character, habits or ethics to destroy mutual respect and affection. Marriage is always a gamble, but with a little foresight and good judgment one can greatly reduce the risks.

There is a decided difference between the state of being "in love," and the sincere love essential for a good marriage. Nearly all romance starts with an attraction of personalities. True love is something that grows by degrees. It is founded upon mutual respect, mutual trust, sympathy, understanding, affection, consideration, and companionship. A marriage is not merely a physical mating, but also a mating of minds and souls. Two people joining their destinies should have common ideals and aspirations. Unless two persons can pull together they will merely hinder each other. Marriage should give a wife security and make the husband feel important as the protector of the home and family.

Love is an emotion but marriage is not a purely emotional experience. It is a problem in adaptation, understanding, and cooperation. Each partner should be able to respect the individuality of the other; yet neither should let his own individualism become a source of conflict.

Marriage is a union of two individuals. The individuals affect the marriage and the marriage affects the character development of the individuals. The institution of marriage is a religious and legal sanction, a rightful concession to the principle of law and order necessary to render harmony to the progress of civilization. Marriage belongs to the sphere of ethics. It is more than just a mating. It is a partnership in living demanding cooperation, respect, and mutual consideration.

The family is the smallest unit of a progressive civilization. Family integrity is the basis of all community law and order. When marriage is taken too lightly, first the family, then the community, and eventually civilization itself degenerates.

The increasing independence of women has changed marriage, but eventually this will be for the better. An intelligent and mature man appreciates a wife who is intelligent and capable.

Many marriages, especially those contracted by persons past middle age, may be made for companionship, prompted by mutual interests and needs rather than by a romantic attraction. Perhaps it would be more correct to say that there is a difference between young love and mature love. Regardless of whether marriage begins with a strong physical and romantic attraction, the satisfaction of the union depends largely upon the mental and spiritual compatibility of the partners. Difference of attitudes in the sphere of ethics, the basis of soul conflicts, causes more discord between a husband and wife than any mere difference of viewpoints, or any lack of sexual compatibility, because it causes such internal suffering.

According to statistics gleaned from many sources of research and investigation, happily married couples will agree in viewpoints but may differ in temperament. Sexual compatibility is not so important as mutual understanding and companionship. Actually, sexual compatibility can be achieved easily by any man and woman who are physically normal and have an attitude toward sex free from disgust, aversion, or sensuality.

In every case of sexual maladjustment that has come to my attention, there has been an abnormality or complex of personality at the root of it; frigidity in a wife, alcoholism in a husband or wife, or neurotic traits of personality in one or both partners. In most cases this deviation of personality existed before the marriage and was not the failure of marital adjustment. The fact that some persons enter marriage with a definite complex against sex indicates that their motive is not biological. Sexual biases are psychological, never physical, except in the case of a deformity.

Here is where the individual horoscope must be considered in astrology.

Assuming that the individuals have a wholesome attitude toward sex, if their horoscopes show a strong attraction, with sufficient mental-emotional-spiritual harmony, as promised by the comparison, a sexual adjustment can be realized. It may take a few weeks, or months, but it can be achieved.

Some of the commonest hazards to a good marriage have been established by various researchers as follows:

- Marriage before the age of 20, especially for the male. At that age few men are ready for the responsibility. Best ages: over 20 for the woman and over 24 for the man.
- Marriage of persons after 40 where the man has never been married. The older bachelor is too fixed in his habits to adjust easily to marriage.
- Marriage between people of widely different ages. More than 15 years difference can be considered a hazard. Many a woman has regretted marriage to a man much older than herself and many a man has regretted marriage to a much younger wife.
- Wide differences of educational, environmental, or social background.
- Parental disapproval and family interferences.

Emotional maturity is listed first by several authorities as a cause of divorce. This is a reason why so many youthful marriages go on the rocks. It is a reasonable finding, for marriage is a project for adults, not children.

We can define emotional maturity as acceptance of responsibility for one's own decisions and mistakes. This brings us back to the fact that marriage is one of the tasks of life. It is a challenge to intelligence,

9

understanding, patience, tact, common sense, loyalty, and faith.

The ability to make a good marriage rests upon the individual attitude toward love, sex, and the responsibilities of life. Choosing a life-mate should be a serious business, but many young people rush into marriage for reasons which seem silly to people of more mature years. One young woman confided to me that she had married her husband because he was like the husband of her sister, whom she idealized. It evidently had not occurred to her that the type of man who suited her sister might not be suitable for her. This particular marriage, incidentally, ended in divorce.

I once asked a younger woman to describe her "ideal" man. She replied that he would be tall, dark, blue-eyed, a neat dresser and polite. Nothing at all about his education, whether he would be intelligent, honest, ambitious, healthy, reliable, or show ability to earn a living. This young woman was not stupid; she simply had not yet learned the difference between personality and character. Romance may begin with an attraction of personalities, but it is character that decides the success of the marriage. We cannot emphasize this too much.

Most marriages, especially between people under forty, start with a romantic attraction. This is compounded by a physical magnetism and personality attraction. Many young people are attracted to their mates because they admire each other's eyes or hair or dance well together, and sometimes, by a streak of good fortune, they find themselves wedded to persons who are right for them. They learn to love each other in the true sense of the word and so make a good marriage.

More often such carelessness in choosing a marriage partner results in misery and ends in divorce. To make a good choice demands maturity of viewpoint and a fine perception of human qualities. Not many young people have this. That is why we have counselors. But it could save time and heartache if young people sought advice before, rather than after marriage. This is where a comparison of horoscopes can be helpful.

In comparing horoscopes for love and marriage we can divide our analysis into two sections.

- Attraction
- Endurability

Attraction

We will begin by analyzing attraction. According to the dictionary, to attract is to "draw by some winning influence: charm, allure, to entice, to win." We can insert parenthetically that some individuals are more attractive to the opposite sex than others, and so attract more opportunities for romance and marriage.

If you are attracted to another person, you are interested, curious, have a friendly feeling, and are disposed to look for favor upon that person. You will pursue and encourage the acquaintanceship. An attraction felt between members of the same sex creates friendship. When two persons of the opposite sex are strongly attracted and feel the pull of animal magnetism, or what we can term the polarity of opposites, we have the basis for romance.

Sometimes such an attraction is superficial and temporary. Many a person has felt attracted to another person of the opposite sex for a brief period and afterward wondered exactly what he or she had seen in that person. Sometimes an attraction is one-sided. Many people mistake pity for love, or are misled by flattery and attention. Sometimes an attraction springs from sheer loneliness.

If real love is to develop, the attraction should be more than a superficial one. In comparing horoscopes we analyze various factors, and the greater the number of aspects of attraction, the stronger will be the attraction. If the student cannot obtain the hour of birth, from which the Ascendant is derived, for both individuals, he can obtain a good judgment from the Ascendant of one horoscope and planets in both. But a comparison based on planets alone, without an Ascendant for either party, would be inadequate, and judgment must be rendered with many reservations. **Most important in judging attraction is the aspect between the Ascendant of one chart and the planets of the other.** This is true not only for marriage but for all comparisons.

Sun, Moon, Venus, or Mars in one horoscope in the sign ascending or descending in the other horoscope is an astrological testimony of a strong attraction. Jupiter,and Mercury are favorable, but less indicative of the emotional appeal that stimulates a romantic attraction between individuals of the opposite sex.

Unless the Ascendant or Descendant of one horoscope combines with the planets of the other by sign, it is doubtful that the attraction would result in marriage. So far as my own experience has been concerned in testing this rule, I would say that an attraction would never result in marriage unless the Ascendant or Descendant of one or both horoscopes is so involved.

It is the Ascendant, symbolizing personality of the individual, that determines the real power or magnetism of the attraction. The Ascendant of one chart in aspect to planets of the other chart **confirms** and **supports** any congeniality and compatibility as read in the aspects formed between planets in the respective horoscopes.

To judge attraction indicated by planets, here is what to look for:

Sun in one horoscope in conjunction, opposition, sextile or trine the

Moon of the other horoscope. It is best for marital harmony if the man's Sun aspects the woman's Moon, but either case indicates a possible attraction. The Sun is the symbol of the masculine and protective quality in an individual. The Moon symbolizes the feminine and domestic instincts. The woman seeks in a husband one who expresses the unconscious masculine (protective and leadership) qualities in her nature. The man seeks in a wife one who expresses the hidden feminine (domestic and dependent) or Moon qualities in his nature. If the woman's Sun aspects the man's Moon, she may incline to dominate him or assume too much leadership. The wife may become ''too bossy,'' a complaint of many an unhappy husband.

The next strongest aspect for judging attraction is found between Mars and Venus. Mars symbolizes the **aggressive**, **amatory** desire nature, and Venus the **passive, yielding** affections. Mars is the (masculine) lover. Venus the (feminine) beloved. Both planets have **sexual significance**, i.e. may indicate the sexual instincts or attitude toward sex and love in the individual. Mars-Venus combinations between charts, therefore, stimulate affection and desire for each other in the individuals.

In all the combinations mentioned in this book, the reference is to the position of one planet in the horoscope of one person as it aspects the second planet named in the horoscope of the other person. Thus, Mars conjunct Venus means the man's Mars conjunct the woman's Venus or vice versa.

Mars conjunct Venus or Mars trine or sextile Venus indicates a stimulating and congenial attraction. Mars opposite or square Venus is a strong physical attraction but there also may be an element of friction in it. There is too much emotion, sometimes jealousy, or repulsion mixed with the attraction. Unless there are points in the two charts which give it a high rating for endurability, such attractions are likely to be shortlived. Sometimes the adverse Mars-Venus aspects indicate a one-sided attraction.

We also can consider as planetary elements indicating attraction between a man and woman:

Venus conjunct, opposite, trine, or sextile Uranus. There is a fascination in this combination; it is very magnetic. If there is such a thing as ''love at first sight,'' Uranus will indicate it in a comparison. Uranus indicates excitement; a sparkling and often unusual or unconventional courtship may result, especially in the case of the conjunction. Uranus conjunct, trine, or sextile the Sun or Moon also can produce a romantic attraction. In the case of the **conjunction** of Uranus to Venus, Sun, or Moon, there may be temptation to indiscretions before marriage.

Venus conjunct, opposite, sextile or trine the Sun or Moon indicates an emotional attraction born of sympathy, social conviviality, and mutual tastes and interests. Mars conjunct, trine or sextile Sun or Moon also can be considered as a favorable aspect of attraction. The reader will note that only in the case of Venus do we include the opposition. Mars in opposition to the Sun or Moon tends to produce irritations which prevent the attraction from being entirely comfortable. And the square, while it may indicate an attraction in some cases, is usually temporary unless there are many other favorable aspects in the comparison to promote endurability.

If potential sexual compatibility can be judged from the comparison, aspects between Mars and Venus, or more important, between the Ascendant of one and Venus, Mars, Sun, or Moon of the other chart, will tell the story.

Not all attractions will or should result in marriage. Some attractions may never get beyond the state of courtship or may end in a broken engagement. In some cases circumstances may hinder the progress of the attachment or individual ideals and inclinations may sever the association before it comes to the marriage stage.

Let us repeat again that there is more to marriage than love and sexual compatibility. If sex were of first importance in marriage, a woman of refinement, education and culture who is strongly sexed, could mate happily with any virile, healthy, decent-looking male, no matter how uncouth and illiterate. But we know that this could never be. Both would be miserable because their basic spiritual, mental, and soul requirements would clash. A woman of culture probably would not be attracted to such a man to begin with. No man or woman can marry beneath his station in life and not regret it. But even sexual satisfaction with a mate of one's own station will not by itself insure a happy marriage. The main cause of divorce is not sexual incompatibility, but serious personal conflicts, financial difficulties, or unresolved family problems.

A further word about attractions: During the adolescent period, roughly between the fourteenth and nineteenth years (this is the Venus cycle of the individual's life, of which we will speak more fully in the section under parent-child relationships), when the biological love nature is being awakened, a young girl or boy may have any number of sweethearts before finally settling the affections upon one individual. This is the "falling in love" period during which the deeper capacity for love is not yet awakened. The average person during that period is too immature to analyze emotions, so can be deceived by his feelings. He is in love with love and with having someone interested in him. He is swept away by passing emotions.

That is why so may youthful marriages end in separation.

The qualities in others that appealed to them in youth no longer attract them in more mature years and, unless the young husband and wife are able to grow up together, their changing interests and ideals may split them apart. They fail to satisfy each other's spiritual needs. Many young people are attracted by their opposites, who have qualities which supply the imbalance in their own natures. In more mature years, having achieved a better rounded development of personality, individuals are more attracted to their similars.

The fact that marriage before the age of twenty-one is considered risky by those who have studied the subject agrees with the esoteric teaching that an individual does not begin to know himself until he is twenty-one. This is when he comes into the Sun cycle of his development. He then is considered adult and should be (though unfortunately not always is) ready for self-responsibility.

According to statistics gleaned from various sources, marriages are more frequent between individuals of different temperament than similar temperaments.

Happily married couples will agree in viewpoints, however. Temperaments may differ, but should be congenial. That is, they should blend or balance each other, not clash. (This is known as polarity). In astrology, temperament is described by the elements: i.e. fire, earth, air, and water categories of the signs.

Aries, Leo, and Sagittarius are fire signs. The earth signs are Taurus, Virgo, and Capricorn. Air signs are Gemini, Libra, and Aquarius, and the water signs are Cancer, Scorpio, and Pisces. People born in the fire signs respond to situations with emotion, desiring direct action in the solving of problems, and tending more to impulse than deliberation. The earth types are motivated by the desire for practical, useful results. They usually have sound common sense, whether they use it or not. The air sign people like to reason things out and generally think before they act. The water sign types are impressionable, sensitive, and intuitive. They incline to wait on circumstances for guidance in solving problems.

The fire and air natures lean toward the extrovert in personality, while the water and earth types incline to be introverts. However, only the entire horoscope of the individual would provide basis for such a pronouncement. Few individuals are definitely one or the other.

The division of personality type, as described by the symbolism of the ''elements'' is further modified by the categories of cardinal, fixed, and mutable. The cardinal signs are Aries, Cancer, Libra, and Capricorn; the fixed signs are Taurus, Leo, Scorpio, and Aquarius; and the mutable signs are Gemini, Virgo, Sagittarius, and Pisces. The cardinal type is enterprising and originating. Progress, for this type, usually is embodied in change and movement. Persons born in the fixed signs are recognized for a fixity of purpose that wins results through sheer persistence. Progress, to them, means acquisition. The mutable type is noted for adaptability and resourcefulness. Progress is associated with achievement rather than with material gains.

Endurability

In analyzing endurability, first consider the respective Suns in the horoscopes. The Sun symbolizes individuality and temperament. If the individuals are pulling in different directions it is a hazard to marital adjustment.

Some years ago, a California judge named Hadaller, who presided over many divorce cases, became interested in the birthdays of the couples who came before him. He found that more couples whose birthdays were from four to six months apart applied for divorce than those whose birthdays were closer together in the year. Astrology cannot afford to ignore any important research that may be helpful. Such findings can be tested and verified or rejected, which is the scientific method of getting at facts.

From cases that have come to my personal attention, I can verify the judge's conclusions, though with some reservations. The four-month-apart birthdays, recognized in astrology as the Sun square Sun, may be able to adjust, but there is always a great deal of tension. There may be conflicting goals, or conflict between individual aspirations, or serious differences of temperament which prohibit complete understanding and agreement. The six-months-apart birthdays, the Sun opposite Sun, are frequently attracted to each other, but like the attraction between those born in the same sign, the couple will adjust easily or not all.

Especially will Suns in square or opposition from fixed signs find many obstacles to understanding and adjustment because the natures lack sufficient flexibility for the necessary give and take of marriage. When a fixed sign Sun marries another fixed sign Sun, it is usually the wife who must make the concessions, and who therefore feels, and may actually be, frustrated by the mate in expressing her individuality. This is particularly true if she is talented and ambitious for personal success.

When marriages in which the Suns are in adverse relationship do result in harmony, the endurability rating will be high. There is enough harmony of personality, along with numerous mutual interests, which offset the conflict indicated by the adverse Sun temperament.

An ideal combination is Sun sextile Sun, especially if the respective Suns are in the same decan of their respective signs. A sextile is better than a trine because there is a blending of temperaments that are somewhat different, yet not hostile as in the case of the Sun square Sun. A husband and wife should complement each other, balance each other, yet not be too much alike, for too much similarity breeds resistance. Nor should they be too different either, for then there is the problem of understanding, accepting, and reconciling their differences.

Not all individuals are fortunate enough to attract or even to meet this ideal. But when they do, and when other requirements for mental-emotional-spiritual harmony are found in the horoscopes, they can consider themselves fortunate.

Individuals born in the same sign are in a class by themselves. Their similarity of type and basic nature will cause them to be either unusually congenial or extremely antagonistic. It all depends upon the other factors in the horoscopes.

Individuals born in signs ruled by the same planet, such as Libra-Taurus, ruled by Venus; Scorpio-Aries, ruled by Mars; Gemini-Virgo, ruled by Mercury; Sagittarius-Pisces, ruled by Jupiter; Capricorn-Aquarius ruled by Saturn (using the old rulership for Scorpio, Pisces, and Aquarius) will be easily adaptable to each other provided the mental-emotional-spiritual requirements are satisfied. Many individuals are attracted to others born in signs in which the respective decans are sub-ruled by the same planets, such as combinations between any two of the following:

- First decan Aries, second decan Gemini, third decan Leo, first decan Scorpio, second decan Capricorn, third decan Pisces, all sub-ruled by Mars.
- Second decan Aries, third decan Gemini, first decan Virgo, second decan Scorpio, third decan Capricorn, all sub-ruled by the Sun.
- Third decan Aries, first decan Cancer, second decan Virgo, third decan Scorpio, first decan Aquarius, all sub-ruled by Venus.
- First decan Taurus, second decan Cancer, third decan Virgo, first decan Sagittarius, second decan Aquarius, all sub-ruled by Mercury.
- Second decan Taurus, third decan Cancer, first decan Libra, second decan Sagittarius, third decan Aquarius, all sub-ruled by the Moon.
- Third decan Taurus, first decan Leo, second decan Libra, third decan Sagittarius, first decan Pisces, all sub-ruled by Saturn.
- First decan Gemini, second decan Leo, third decan Libra, first decan Capricorn, second decan Pisces, all sub-ruled by Jupiter.

The above rulership designations follow the Chaldean system which I have found to be quite reliable in both personality interpretation and comparisons.

In such combination there will be a similarity of viewpoint or attitude in the approach to life and its problems which helps the individuals build a life together, even though in some cases the temperaments are conflicting.

However, regardless of the position of the respective Suns, we need other astrological factors to judge endurability and here we come again to the link between the Ascendants and the planets in the two horoscopes.

Under attraction we analyzed the planets of one horoscope as they fit into the Ascendant or Descendant of the other horoscope. In the following we will consider the Ascendant and planetary rulers of Ascendant as they compare in the two horoscopes. And, as previously stated, unless there are combinations present of the type we will now enumerate, the couple may not marry at all despite any attraction between them.

Through the Ascendant we read love and affection. The Descendant symbolizes the marriage bond, the responsibility of one partner to the other.

- **Ruler of Ascendant of one partner is in the sign ascending in the other's chart.** Example: Aquarius rises in one chart. Ruler is Uranus. Uranus is in Sagittarius in the other chart and Sagittarius is in the sign ascending in this chart.

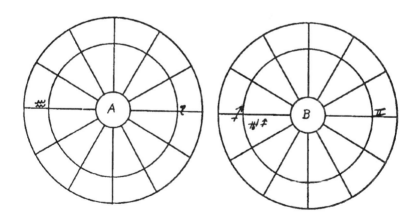

- **Ruler of Descendant of one partner is in the sign ascending in the other.** Example: Libra is on the Descendant of one chart. Ruler is Venus. Venus is in Capricorn in the other chart and Capricorn is the sign ascending in this chart.

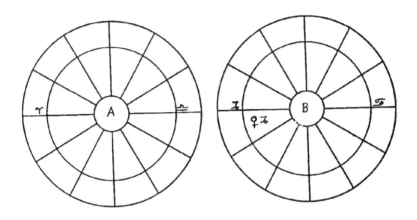

- **Ruler of Ascendant or Descendant of horoscope A will be the same or opposite sign in horoscope B.** Example: Taurus is on Descendant of one chart. Venus is ruler. Venus is in Scorpio in the other chart (thus being in ascending sign of horoscope A).

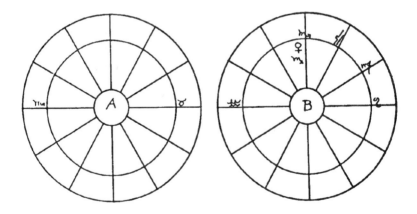

Or, to give another example: Mars, ruler of Ascendant of chart A is in Taurus (sign descending of chart A) in chart B.

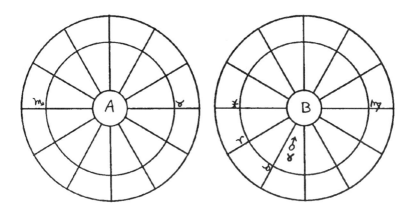

- **Rulers of Ascendants or Descendants of both horoscopes are in the same sign.** Example: Capricorn rises in horoscope A; its ruler, Saturn, is in Gemini, Taurus rises in horoscope B, and Venus, its ruler, is in Gemini.

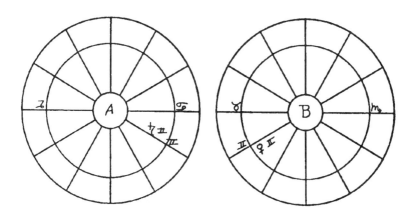

Or: Ruler of Descendant of Chart A is Moon in Pisces. Ruler of Descendant of B is Venus in Pisces.

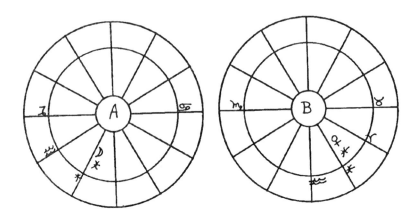

- **Rulers of rising signs or Descendants are in signs opposite in the respective horoscopes.** Example: In chart A Taurus rises with Venus, its ruler, in Virgo. Gemini rises in the other chart with Mercury, its ruler, in Pisces.

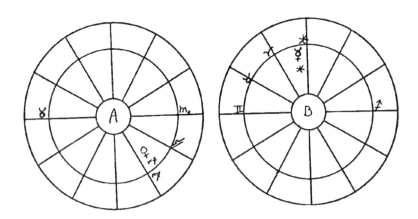

- **Ruler of Ascendant of one horoscope and ruler of Descendant of other horoscope are in the same sign.** Example: Cancer rises in chart A. The Moon, ruling Cancer, is in Gemini. Aries is on the Descendant of chart B and Mars, its ruler, is in Gemini.

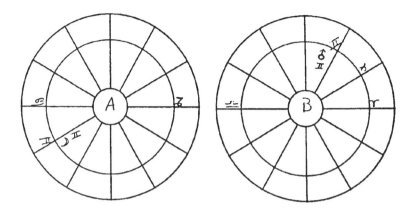

- **Ruler of one Ascendant and ruler of the other Descendant are in opposite signs.** Example: Taurus rises with Venus, its ruler, in Capricorn in chart A. Sagittarius is on the Descendant of chart B, and its ruler, Jupiter, is in Cancer.

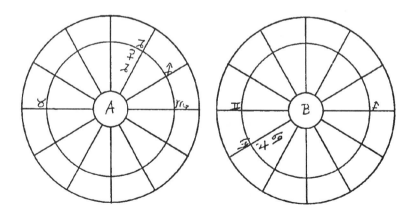

- **Both Ascendants, or the Ascendant of one chart and Descendant of other are ruled by the same planets.** Example:
Aries rising in one horoscope, Scorpio rising or on the Descendant of the other horoscope, both ruled by Mars.
Taurus and Libra Ascendants or Ascendant-Descendant, both ruled by Venus.
Gemini-Virgo Ascendant or Ascendant-Descendant, both ruled by Mercury.
Sagittarius-Pisces, Ascendants or Ascendant-Descendant, both ruled by Jupiter.
Capricorn-Aquarius, Ascendants or Ascendant-Descendant, both ruled by Saturn.
Note: The old system of rulership is used in the last two cases, although we also consider Neptune and Uranus as rulers of Pisces and Aquarius respectively, as can be noted by other examples given elsewhere.
- **The same sign or opposite signs rising in both charts.** Example:
Aries rising in both charts, or Aries rising in one horoscope and Libra rising in the other, and so on with Taurus-Scorpio, Gemini-Sagittarius, Cancer-Capricorn, Leo-Aquarius, Virgo-Pisces.
- **Another excellent sign of understanding and compatibility occurs where rulers of respective Sun signs are in the partner's Sun sign.** Example: Sun in Gemini, and Sun in Cancer; Mercury, which rules Gemini, is in Cancer in the Gemini's chart; Moon, which rules Cancer, is in Gemini in the Cancer's chart.

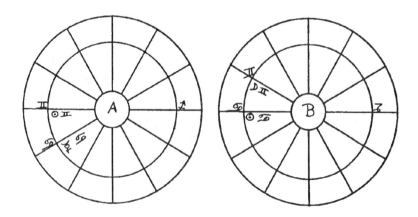

It is an added point in favor of compatibility and endurability if the ruling planet of the two ascendants, or of Ascendant and Descendant are in conjunction, sextile, or trine. Oppositions between Sun, Moon, or the benefics also would be considered favorable.

An added point for endurability is found when one of the Moon's Nodes in one chart is conjunct a planet in the other chart, though this has no meaning as far as personality factors are concerned.

Balance in Temperament and Type

Another important check for endurability is made in the division of planets into the categories of fire, earth, air, water (temperament tendency), and cardinal, fixed, mutable (type). In the individual horoscope one may find the planets distributed in many ways, sometimes evenly; again there may be a majority of planets in one element or quality. In comparing two horoscopes, adjustment will be easier, and therefore more conducive to agreement and endurability, if there is a good balance between the two horoscopes. Fire and air balance perfectly; earth and water balance perfectly. Fire can adjust well to earth, but is discordant with water. Air adjusts well enough with water, but is discordant to earth.

If partners have a majority of planets in the same element there is apt to be too much similarity in temperament and this can cause tension or conflict. The same with the type category. A majority of planets in cardinal signs in both horoscopes, for instance, can produce conflict over questions of leadership or authority. If a majority of planets are in fixed signs in both, there may be obstinacy in both which makes agreement difficult should they oppose each other in major questions.

Here are some examples of good balance:

	Husband	Wife
Fire	1	4
Earth	3	2
Air	5	2
Water	1	2
Cardinal	2	1
Fixed	5	2
Mutable	3	7
Fire	1	3
Earth	3	-
Air	4	3
Water	2	4
Cardinal	2	2

Fixed	5	2
Mutable	3	6

Mental Agreement

Mental agreement is indicated by aspects formed between Mercury and Moon in respective horoscopes, or between Mercury and Mercury. A conjunction, sextile, or trine aspect between Mercury-Moon and/or Mercury-Mercury denotes harmony of ideas, interests, and viewpoints, or ability to see the other's point of view in case of any difference of opinion. Such aspects also indicate stimulus of mind on mind, encourage mutual interests, and establish companionship.

An opposition between Mercury-Moon or Mercury-Mercury can be judged as favorable but is not as good as the conjunction, sextile, or trine. A square between Mercury-Moon is not seriously conflicting, but denotes mild differences of ideas and individual interests. A square between Mercury-Mercury, however, can be very trying for mental adjustment and mutual understanding and agreement. This is especially true if the two Mercuries are in fixed signs and if there is no aspect between Mercury-Moon or Mercury-Sun between the charts to assist understanding.

A conjunction, sextile, or trine between Mercury and one of the luminaries helps mutual understanding and ability to come to agreements. Adjustments can be made harmoniously when the reasoning mind (Mercury) of one partner is in tune with the perceptions and receptivity or feelings (Moon), or the creative instincts or inherent nature and ideals (Sun) of the other partner. Favorable aspects between Jupiter and Moon, or Jupiter and Mercury also aid understanding and can stimulate mutual interest.

Position of Saturn

The position of Saturn in one horoscope as it falls in the other's horoscope also must be considered, for Saturn symbolizes duty, responsibility and the disciplinary or limiting as well as stabilizing qualities in one individual as they would affect the other. Saturn in one of the angles, especially if the woman's Saturn falls in the husband's first, tenth, seventh, or fourth (relatively powerful in the order named) is difficult to work with. She may have a tendency to limit or thwart him in his ambitions, or to be critical or demanding, or expect too much of him. The responsibilities she brings or imposes upon him can be a drawback.

The husband's Saturn in the wife's first, tenth, seventh, or fourth is restricting and sometimes frustrating. If the husband's Saturn is also in square aspect to either Sun, Mars, Moon, Venus, or Jupiter in the wife's chart, it is more so. Considering, however, that the man should be head of the household and the provider and that his ambitions (work, career, profession) should be put before the wife's, his Saturn in one of the angles of her horoscope is not quite such a handicap to the congeniality and prosperity of the couple as when the reverse is true. It may cause some friction (or problem of adjustment) in either case, since what upsets one partner can upset the other by reaction, because individuals living together in the intimacy of marriage do not easily conceal their feelings or emotions and moods from the other.

Wherever the Saturn of one chart falls in the other horoscope it tends to crystallize or limit, or denotes a type of duty-responsibility that must be accepted, or problems that have to be solved. Saturn emphasizes duty or obligation in that sphere. For example, suppose Saturn in the husband's chart falls in the eleventh house of his wife's chart. He may restrict her social life or criticize her friends. He could be jealous of her interest in them or might impose social obligations upon her for his own purposes. The duties he brings into the marriage will prove an obstacle to her in realizing some of her hopes and wishes, which she perforce may have to set aside for the harmony of the union.

We have to put up with Saturn someplace! Wherever it is it will mean lessons to be learned and problems of adjustment; so in comparing horoscopes, look to Saturn and decide if its disciplines can be endured. In some cases, the discipline or responsibility of Saturn may be a benefit to character development. A wife's Saturn in the husband's second house may help their economic fortunes, for she will either help him to save, or will curtail any tendency to extravagance or carelessness in money matters that lurks in his nature. Or she may help strengthen his sense of responsibility along economic lines.

How to Compare the Horoscopes

To make a comparison for love and marriage:
- Analyze first the quality and degree of attraction as outlined in the Attraction section in this chapter.
- Analyze the potentials for endurance of the union as outlined in the Endurability section.
- Compare the division of planets as to temperament and type for balancing natural expression in disposition and character.
- Analyze the aspects between Sun, Moon, and Mercury for harmony of viewpoint as indicated in the Mental Agreement section.
- Judge the influence of the Saturn of one partner as it falls in the horoscope of the other.
- Make a list of all the aspects formed by all the planets and luminar-

ies between the two horoscopes and look up the interplanetary interpretations in Part Two of this book. This will tell you how each planet (for the sake of word simplicity we will include Sun and Moon as planets) in one horoscope will react upon the other.

This reveals how a certain instinct, feeling, tendency of emotion, trait of personality or character (as indicated by a planet of one individual) affects an instinct, feeling, tendency of emotion, or trait of personality or character in the other individual. After this has been read, make a list of all the favorable aspects and a separate list of the testing or discordant aspects. If the harmonious aspects are more numerous than the discordant ones the outlook for the success of the marriage can be judged as favorable.

The discordant oppositions, testing conjunctions and squares, however few in number they are, cannot be dismissed. Because—and this is the crux of the whole comparison—the congeniality and adaptability to each other of the individuals and the success in working out their problems will be determined by the way in which the two individuals handle these testing aspects.

These are the conflicts, the points on which there is liability to misunderstanding, disagreement or tension, or difficulty of compromise or cooperation. They are the tests of patience and understanding and coming to agreement or finding a basis of working together. They are the aspects which test the disposition, or the character, the capabilities, faith, and even the spiritual integrity of an individual. The harmonious aspects indicate the means by which understanding and agreement can help the couple resolve the qualities that tend to arouse conflict between them. So, in a sense, these testing or problem-creating aspects can be a means of improving and strengthening the characters and bringing out capabilities in both.

When, however, the testing aspects are more numerous than the favorable aspects, and especially if many unfavorable aspects are found between malefics, the individuals are likely to bring out the worst instead of the best sides in each other. Thus, affection and love are not likely to survive the tests of cohabitation.

In some marriages one partner may be very contented while the other is but mildly happy or sometimes even miserable. But if there is real love and affection, if a good give-and-take exists between husband and wife, and there is a mutual consideration and unselfishness, the partners should derive equal satisfaction from the union.

Married couples have much to learn from each other. Sometimes, unsuspected personality faults that were not previously observed in an individual crop up after marriage.

Now, suppose a couple is already married, and has been married for a number of years. A marriage comparison can help them understand many puzzling factors of their union and perhaps enable them to become more reconciled to each other. It can even save a marriage that is in danger of breaking up. Many problems, discords, and tensions might be dissolved in this understanding. And if the going still seems hard, it may be well to consider the words of Swedenborg, who wrote in his book *Conjugal Love*:

> When marriages are unhappy, or sympathy is imperfect, it does not necessarily follow that either of the partners is to blame; nor are we to think that such marriages are without benefit to the individuals concerned. It may be that the trials incidental to an ill-assorted marriage are sometimes an important means of strengthening and refining the character.

However, there are some cases in which the Soul evolvement of the individual would be retarded rather than advanced by an unhappy union. In such cases, if an individual is unable to find compensation for an unhappy marriage by some form of self-expression, or by a self-fulfilling service to humanity, and if no one can be hurt by it, it may be best to sever the union.

Let us not forget that in marriage comparisons, as in all other comparisons, we are considering the reaction of individuals upon each other. We must consider the two horoscopes separately, too. The man's or woman's potential for making a success of marriage will be indicated by aspects to Venus or by aspects of the Moon and Sun.

Moon in the woman's chart indicates her ability as a homemaker, The Sun in the man's chart indicates his ability to be a good provider, protector, father, or head of the household.

Suggested Reading

The Challenge of Marriage, Rudolf Dreikurs, M.D., Duell, Sloan and Peace

Marriage is on Trial, Judge Sbarbaro, MacMillan Co.

Marriage, Before and After, Dr. Paul Popenoe, Sc. D., Wilfred Funk, Inc.

What Life Should Mean to You (chapter entitled Love and Marriage), Alfred Adler, Blue Ribbon Books

For People Under Pressure (Chapter 8), David Harold Fink, M.D., Simon and Schuster.

Chapter 3
Parent-Child Relationships

Whether recognized or not, the principal job of the parent is to prepare the child for adulthood. In giving the child affection and protection, parents help the child build emotional security, and through proper discipline teach the child the meaning of cooperation and responsibility. Thus they steer the child into habits of living which build a self-reliant, well-balanced individual.

Complete harmony in a parent-child relationship is made difficult because of the age difference ("the generation gap"). When a person becomes a parent he tends to forget how he behaved as a child or even to remember that he once was one. Grown-ups need to be reminded that children are not just "underdone" adults, but individuals with distinct personalities of their own; that their personalities and characters are going through a process of formation; and that this formative process is affected by their reaction to their parents, the family, and home environment.

Proverbs 22:6 says: "Train up a child in the way he should go and when he is old he will not depart from it." Psychology, which teaches that the first seven years are most important in establishing behavior patterns, agrees with this. This is the period when personality habits are formed and when behavioral tendencies or complexes take root. In astrology, this the Moon cycle of individual development.

During the course of my life, I have known many parents and have observed how they managed their children. I have met many loving parents (most parents do love their offspring), and many intelligent, well-intentioned, and conscientious parents, but few parents who balanced love and affection with common sense efficiency in raising their young. Despite all the child psychology books, most parents are either too permissive, too strict, too protective, or too neglectful. They still react to and manage their children from the springboard of their own emotions and personalities. They either want to dominate or they are too possessive, or maybe too indulgent and lax. In determining the future of the child most parents are motivated by what they want for the child, not necessarily what may be most suitable for the child. They force the child into some mold of their own design, instead of studying the child impersonally to bring out his best qualities and abilities.

Many parents are inconsistent, which confuses a child and affects his response to the parent. For instance, a father I knew, when in an irritable mood, would become angry with his son for some slight cause, but at other times would laugh at the child for the identical misdemeanor or piece of mischief. Naturally the child became confused as to whether that action was acceptable or not.

Another point that parents often overlook is that their children are likely to have one or more tendencies of personality found in their own natures. When parents observe their own shortcomings in their children they may forget that the child is simply following predispositions. If that trait is not desirable the best way for the parent to discourage it in the child is to eradicate it in himself. In other words, a parent must set an example in those meritorious qualities he would like his child to emulate or develop. Children tend to imitate their parents, a few of their habits at least, and more often than not in those which are least admirable.

A parent should remember that he is the child's first teacher. He begins to teach his child from the first moment the child shows an awareness of his environment, and that may be as early as the second month of infancy. At this early stage we speak of teaching more accurately as conditioning, to use a term popular with psychologists. Conditioning is the establishing (or training) of habits. First come the functional, physical habits of eating, sleeping, and training in habits of elimination. These condition the infant to become a social human being instead of an animal. Later on, when the child becomes more aware of his surroundings, his powers of observation are brought into play and his perceptions—sight, hearing, touch—develop so that learning ability grows rapidly. When he begins to talk, his understanding and receptivity to learning becomes still keener. At these stages the parents can teach the child to prepare his mind for the instruction he will receive when he enters school. The best students are those who have received a certain amount of preschool training. While it is never a good idea to urge the child too fast for his years and intelligence, he should be given all the instruction he shows any inclination and ability to absorb. That most children are eager to learn is plainly indicated by all the questions they ask, and things they try to do.

The first important quality to instill in a child is obedience; not blind submission to the arbitrary will of a strong, more physically powerful authority, but obedience that springs from a desire to please. The parent's task here is to win obedience and cooperation from the child without destroying the child's natural individual initiative, curiosity, and aggressive spirit. Such obedience can be won only by love and patient instruction and explanation. Children want to know the reasons "why" they are to do, or not to do, this or that.

This understanding is seldom acquired in one lesson, because children, like many grown-ups, learn only through mistakes and mishaps. But once children understand the relationship between cause and effect they will obey more readily. Judicious correction and punishment is often necessary. The "let the child do as he pleases" school of child training is decidedly passé and child psychologists now realize that the adage "spare the rod and spoil the child" contains the essence of wisdom.

Parents should try to understand the nature of children and not worry over every little element of misbehavior. Parents can turn normal youngsters into "problem children" by trying to "psychoanalyze" every action of the child. The main thing is to love the child, and make plain what you want him to do and why. Then be patient, use imagination, and apply your sense of humor.

Another point important for the parent to recognize in raising a child is the stages of growth through which the child goes, recognized by astrologers as cycles of development. A parent should not expect too much of a child for his stage of growth. From the first year to about the fourth he is in the Moon cycle. During this period he develops personality habits and powers of observation, becomes aware of and interested in his surroundings, reaches out to understand and experience things through the senses—through taste, touch, smell, sight, and hearing. Taste, touch, and sight are the first senses developed. That is why the child wants to put everything into his mouth; taste is one of the faculties by which he recognizes and understands many things. Then he develops recognition by smell and hearing. In the Moon cycle, the reflexes are mainly those of feeling and sensation. When the hearing sense begins to coordinate with the thinking processes and when the child begins to recognize people, sounds and the meaning of words, and to compare things, then we note signs of mentality (Mercury) at work.

With the speech comes a more "give and take" relationship with the parent. The first seven years are most important in shaping the child's personality development and his attitude toward parents affects this.

From about the fourth to twelfth year the child's growth can be described by Mercury. This is the period during which the normal child grows rapidly, physically as well as mentally. The child is learning, beginning to discover his interests, talents, and abilities for mental expression. He talks more and thinks more. He may show numerous interests which help the parent discern special talents, though perhaps in a very general way.

At this stage the parent should allow the child to experiment in using tools and encourage him to try anything that arouses his interest, provided it is not physically dangerous. However transitory it may be, it helps the child to discover special aptitudes. These later aid him in the choice of a suitable vocation, or may become a source of a satisfying hobby.

At the onset of puberty and during adolescence, the parent-child relationship enters a new phase. From the twelfth to about the nineteenth year the child goes through the Venus cycle of his development. This is the period of adolescence when the glands are changing the child into a man or woman, biologically speaking. There will be many emotional conflicts during this stage because one side of the personality is biologically adult, awakening the urge for independence, while the other side still wishes (subconsciously at least) to remain a sheltered child. This is a very difficult period for the child who finds himself with desires that he has never before experienced and does not fully comprehend. It is during this period that romantic and sexual impulses are awakened. This is a critical period for many parents in the management of children. However, where love and confidence exist between child and parent, the transition the child is now making will not be too difficult for him.

When the young person enters the twenty-first year he comes into the Sun cycle of his life. At this stage he should be ready for self-management and self-responsibility, and if his early training has been adequate, he will be. He may still need the advice and guidance of parents (or some adult in whom he has confidence) but it should be more the counsel of a friend than that of a person of authority.

At this stage the parent should be ready to relinquish his jurisdiction over the child, and it should not hurt him if his son or daughter shows tendencies that appear to be out of character to the parents. It is at this stage that a person begins to exhibit his individualism, and discovers his real self. If his early training has given him foundations of good ethics, education, and preparation for self-responsibility, the parent should be able to trust the young adult not to make any drastic mistakes.

I have heard parents remark of a young son or daughter: "I don't know what's got into Junior; he never behaved this way before.'' Astrologers know that children can change as they grow up and especially as they leave the teens and enter the twentieth year, or Sun cycle. But if the parent understands the stage of growth the child is going through, any changes of personality will not seem inconsistent to him. The meaning of it can be read in the child's horoscope from the position of the Moon, Mercury, Venus, and then the Sun.

The reaction of parent and child upon each other must be considered, too. The aspects between parents' planets to tje child's Moon in the first cycle, the aspects between parent's planets and the child's Mercury in the Mercury cycle, and so on, will aid the parent to understand his probable effect upon the child and the child's tendency of reaction to the parent at each stage of the child's growth.

To compare horoscopes of parent and child, compare the position of the Ascendants with planets and the planetary aspects between the charts. If the harmonious aspects are more numerous, the parent-child relationship will be generally serene. But if the conflicting aspects are the most numerous, there can be tensions and difficulty. Most difficult are the squares between malefic planets. The conjunction of Sun and Mars, or Saturn and Mars, Saturn and Moon, or Saturn and Sun, also tend to create problems in parent-child adjustment.

In cases where there are many tensions and problems of adjustment, the parent should take pains to understand the child and to lay aside his own prejudices and preferences regarding what he wants his child to do or become. Training the child will never be an impossible task if the parent loves the child, gives the child affection and assurance of his love, and is firm in teaching the child the moral and ethical standards which will fit him for good citizenship in his adult years. More than that no parent can do.

Sometime the horoscope of one parent is more harmonious with the horoscope of a child than the other. In such a case, the most harmonious parent can help the other parent to understand the child, and he or she may be better able to reason with the child, guide him, and help him understand the parent who seems conflicting. Care should be taken, of course, that this more harmonious parent does not overindulge or spoil the child. Parents should always strive for cooperation in raising a child, for if they contradict each other's instructions, the child is sure to take advantage of it, and play one parent against the other. If the child who discovers this trick is not made confused and insecure by the difference between his parents' instructions, he may become willful and disobedient, hostile to the parent who is trying to help him, dominating the parent who has indulged him. This creates a serious family problem that is bad for both parents as well as for the child.

Suggested Reading

Children are People, Emily Post, Funk and Wagnalls Co.

Help to Help Your Child Grow Up, Angelo Patri, Rand, McNally Co.

As the Twig is Bent, Leslie B. Hohman, M.D., Macmillan Co.

Growing Together, Rhoda W. Boemeister, D. Appleton-Century Co., Inc.

What Life Should Mean to You (Adolescence), Alfred Adler, Blue Ribbon Books.

Chapter 4
Family Relationships

Brothers and Sisters

In his book *What Life Should Mean to You,* Alfred Adler discusses the way in which personality traits can be developed in children of the same family as a result of their reactions upon each other. Testing his theories proves them to be accurate in a majority of cases. Understanding and wise parents will be able to forestall or correct any unfortunate personality traits threatened.

Not only the child's reaction to his parents and environment affects the development of his personality, but also his attitude toward other children in the family. It is a matter of adjustment. As a rule the first child finds it more difficult to accept and adjust to the second child born to his parents than does the second child in accepting the first. The oldest and youngest of a large family are most apt to develop personality one-sidedness or inferiority feelings. The "only" child, who receives all the parental attention, is sometimes overindulged, but he does not always develop in the spoiled-child pattern. Often, the youngest of a large family is more spoiled than the "only" child.

In a large family it is up to the parents to help the sisters and brothers adjust to each other rationally. A certain amount of rivalry or bickering is normal, children being what they are. Usually it is good-natured, and seldom malicious or prolonged. Parents should mainly watch for signs of jealousy and tale-bearing, for these are danger signals which can lead to forming unfavorable traits in the child.

Children within two or three years of age usually adjust to each other more easily than when there is a wider age difference. This is because of the divergences of interests as well as differing stages of development they are in.

Horoscopes of children in the family can be compared in the same manner as other horoscopes are compared. The information, of course, will be worth more to the parents than to the children. The purpose of such comparisons usually will be to help children get along well together should there be signs of hostility. Also, after another child has come into the family, the parents may observe undesirable traits developing in a child which were not in evidence earlier. The parents should help the child to overcome such traits, though they should never take sides. In fact, it is usually by showing a preference for one child above another, or by setting up one child as an example to the other, that most of the jealousies, resentments, or hostile qualities formed by one child toward another in the family are started.

In the case of sisters and/or brothers of adult years, a comparison can be used by them if any business or other partnership or sharing of home is contemplated.

Not all sisters and/or brothers are naturally harmonious, even though they do come from the same parents. In most cases a bond of sentiment and shared memories of childhood will bind them together in growing up and, as a rule, children of the same family will exhibit many similar traits and interests which establish compatibility.

It can be noticed in studying family horoscopes how often Ascendants are in the same or opposite signs. Or perhaps the Ascendant or Descendant of one child and the Sun or Moon of the other will show what we might call a family pattern. Often, too, planets will occupy the same or opposite signs, or the same sign type (cardinal, fixed, mutable) or planetary aspects will be repeated. As a rule, these family members retain their association with each other throughout their lives.

Sometimes, however, there will be a member of a family so different from the rest that there is little sympathy and desire to cling to the family group in any way.

Any other family connections, such as aunts, uncles, cousins, or in-laws, can be analyzed for mutual understanding and harmony by following the same rules for horoscope comparisons given previously.

Chapter 5
Friendships

When we analyze friendships there are not so many factors of the horoscope to be considered. Friends are seldom together for long periods of time unless they live together. In this case, the horoscopes should be analyzed more as a business partnership in which sharing of expenses and responsibilities are involved.

Two individuals will be able to build a friendship on but a few mutual interests, since it should be easy in the interests of harmony to avoid argument or conflict over any differences of opinion that might arise. Differences of temperament or personality between individuals are not so apt to cause conflicts in friendships as they do in marriage, parent-child relationships or other family relationships.

Friendships are most sympathetic and lasting, however, if there are a maximum of favorable aspects in the comparison. Attraction and mutual interests which ensure social congeniality are shown through the Ascendants, Venus, Moon, Mercury, Jupiter, and Sun aspects.

People of gregarious nature and those who have a wide range of interests and activities will attract many different types of friends. One friend appeals to one facet of his personality, while another friend appeals to a different side of his nature. No individual should confine himself to but one friend, for this is fair neither to the friend nor to oneself. The person who ties himself to one friend denies himself the stimulus he can get from many different minds; he also tends to impose upon or absorb his one friend too much. People who do this are demonstrating a possessive and selfish nature.

Friends must be earned and cultivated. You cannot expect people to be interested in you unless you are interested in them. Friendship is reciprocal. A good friendship is founded on mutual confidence. If you do not feel that you trust a person, do not make a confidant of him. A person who would betray a confidence is not a sincere friend. Friendship, like other relationships of life, requires a lot of tolerance, patience, tact and humor, as well as loyalty and willingness to be helpful.

Be friendly to everyone, for the impersonal love that is circulated by friendship is infectious. It breeds "good will towards men." Be neighborly in your contacts with people whom you see frequently, even if you do not expect to cultivate them as intimates. You never know where or when you may meet someone with whom a mutually encouraging and beneficial association can be formed.

We tend to dislike people who arouse negative reactions such as fear, envy, resentment, criticism, rebellion, disapproval, ethical, or moral differences, or those who offend our sense of justice, our pride, or who are critical, fault-finding or selfish. You can be courteous yet indifferent to those who arouse no common interests or pleasant reactions. If you seriously and strenuously dislike a person, look within yourself for the reason, for that person could be exhibiting traits which you, yourself, possess to some degree. It is a psychological fact that we often see our own shortcomings in others. "Judge not that ye be not judged."

Suggested Reading

Understanding Other People, Stuart Palmer, Thomas Y. Crowell Company.

Chapter 6
Business or Professional Partnerships

Comparison of the planets can be made according to the rules given in Part Two of this book, but there are a few points that should be emphasized here.

The main object of a business partnership is for material gain. Economic factors being of prime importance, the position of Jupiter in the comparison chart is of special importance. Saturn also is important because it symbolizes the duties, responsibilities, and fulfillment of obligations, whether monetary or of service, labor, or distribution.

Jupiter in conflicting aspect with Jupiter, or Saturn in conflicting aspect to Saturn will indicate serious problems or differencesof opinion in handling matters which these planets describe.

Saturn in testing aspect to Jupiter, especially by square, denotes problems in financial management or in the disposal of profits. Business partnerships being described by the seventh house in a horoscope, the ruling planets of the respective Dscendants should be in harmonious aspect for the best cooperation and agreement. A conjunction between the Moon's Ndes in one chart and a planet in the other or with the Acendant of the other horoscope can be taken into consideration in judging the endurability of the partnership.

In most partnerships, one individual will usually be the more aggressive and assume the most leadership and responsibility, playing a dominant role. If both are aggressive and of very positive or strong willed natures, there will be conflict unless duties are clearly defined and faithfully followed.

Other Business Associations

In an organization composed of many individuals, executives, assistants and workers, there is apt to be such diversity of planetary combinations that it would be difficult, if not impossible, to isolate factors that would ensure complete harmony between all its members. As a rule, if the position of planets for birth dates of a group of men, women, or men and women, can be ascertained, it will be found that there are sign combinations linking them. For example, in one company, two of the top executives were born with Sun in Aquarius; the pesident was born in Capricorn with two planets in Aquarius; another top man was born with Sun in Sagittarius with three Capricorn planets, and so on.

In all large organizations, the horoscope of the president or administrative official will be the dominating one, and will influence, if not completly determine, the success or failure of the enterprise. This will be so unless he is a mere figurehead, since he will have control of nearly all situations that arise and make the final decisions, be they wise or foolish. He will have the largest responsibility. The people who work for him will have to do most of the "adjusting," although the chief executive might often listen to advice. The main point is that if he attracts into his aura people whose horoscopes conflict with his, they will have to subdue their antagonistic qualities, or the association is not likely to last long. In the case of an employee such as a secretary, clerk, cashier, salesman or mechanic, comparisons can be made between charts of the worker and his immediate supervisor or the manager of the department for which he works.

Anyone using horoscopes to choose an employee should, of course, consider the applicant's qualifications for the job before a comparison is made.

In making comparisons, particular attention should be given to the positions of Mars, Saturn, Moon, Mercury, and Sun. Where any of these planets are in frictional aspect between the horoscopes there is likely to be a problem of adjustment between the individuals.

In huge organizations where there are many separate departments, comparisons might be made between the supervisor or person at the head of a department and each worker under him. As a rule the worker's fitness for the job will be decided by his personality as well as his intelligence, training, and experience. People who work in or with large groups should be adaptable enough to get along with all sorts of individuals, to be casually friendly for the sake of a good relationship, to be willing to cooperate, and so on. Sometimes a worker will be hired whose disposition and personality creates discord and it is up to the supervisor to handle this situation, or to dismiss the trouble-making worker for the sake of departmental harmony.

Usually executives and supervisors will more readily put up with a little slowness or inefficiency in a worker than with disagreeable personality traits. One who gets along well with his co-workers will be more willing to heed the advice and suggestions of the boss and to take orders from him than will the worker who does not get along well with his fellows. In the long run he makes the better employee and in time will surpass a more brilliant or experienced worker who does not get along well with co-workers.

In short, in this, as in all relationships of life, we come back to the proposition that the ability to get along harmoniously with one's fellow man is the most important factor of success and happiness.

Part Two

Chapter 7
Planetary Keywords

As a prelude to the following exposition, it may be helpful to enumerate the psychological urges and personality tendencies symbolized by the Sun, Moon, and planets. These provide keywords for comparison between planets in two horoscopes. Students can then better understand, and even add to, the interpretations given in this section.

Sun

The power urge. Vitalizing, life-giving force. Radiation. Symbol of masculinity, paternity, authority, and creative ability. Denotes ambition, pride, a protecting, healing, encouraging, warming influence. The Sun creates, achieves, elevates, honors, governs, sustains, dominates, promotes, and negotiates.

Moon

Domestic, family, serving urge. The subconscious or subjective mind. Receptive, responding, reflecting in effect. Symbol of femininity, fecundity, maternity, disposition, feeling, mood, routine, submission, adaptation, obedience, sensitivity, intuition, visual and mental perception, sensation, imagination, hygiene. The Moon sees, perceives, observes, reflects, visualizes, imagines, imitates, serves, eats, drinks, sleeps, absorbs, feels, senses.

Mercury

Intellectual urge. The conscious, objective mind. Symbol of mentality, ideas and interests, curiosity and capacity for learning, reason, analysis, communication, distribution, self-expression, discrimination, selection, judgment. Mercury narrates, talks, argues, debates, writes, analyzes, memorizes, reports, studies, learns, travels, sells, distributes, interprets, listens, reflects, meditates, expresses with the hands.

Venus

Social urge. Balancing, harmonizing, peacemaking influence. Symbol of affection, sentiment, sympathy, friendship, personal or sexual love, romance, beauty, order, agreement, fidelity, pleasure, art, music, rhythm, culture and refinement, conviviality, courtesy, manners, tact, attractiveness, taste, the responsive attitude in love and courtship. Venus loves, praises, beautifies, perfects, amuses, entertains, sings and dances, pacifies, placates, gives, modifies, balances, sympathizes, adorns, decorates, embellishes.

Mars

Aggressive urge. Stimulating and energizing force. Symbol of desire, action, initiative, leadership, executive ability, physical courage, impulse, industry, enterprise, adventure, push and drive, self-will, resistance, combativeness, accident; the aggressive attitude in love and courtship, jealousy, vindictiveness. Mars leads instigates, engineers, disputes, provokes, executes, adventures, dares, irritates, defends, offends, protects, promotes, exploits, moves, challenges, rebels, burns, inflames, speeds.

Jupiter

Benevolent and protective urge. Protective, expanding influence. Symbol of opportunity, increase, rewards, abundance, generosity, tolerance, charity, philanthropy, ethics, faith, confidence, idealism, aspiration, honor, justice and mercy, loyalty, joviality, fair play, prophecy. Jupiter inflates, benefits, protects, comforts, assists, enlarges, magnifies, spends, donates, speculates, laughs, cures, inspires, encourages, counsels, philosophizes.

Saturn

Security or safety urge. Consolidating, crystallizing, conserving, stabilizing, maturing, disciplinary, limiting effect. Symbol of duty, work, responsibility, government, obstacles, endurance, stoicism, persistence, delay, worry, fear, seriousness, solemnity, resentment, envy, anxiety, penury, saving, retaining, deflating, chilling, freezing. Saturn denotes criticism, ignorance, pessimism, negativeness, memory, history, foundations, sorrow, wisdom through experience, age, death. Saturn weighs endures, persists, burdens, builds, instructs, administrates, organizes, conserves, supports, saves, hoards, binds, confines, denies, delays, discredits, discourages, chastises, hesitates, withholds, frustrates, deflates, chills, inhibits, punishes, hates, resents, criticizes, condemns, prohibits.

Uranus

Freedom urge. Exciting, uprooting, awakening effect. Electrical energy. Symbol of awakening and evolving of higher consciousness. Rebellion, individualism, freedom, altruism, the unpredictable, originality, invention, experimentation, the new and unusual, unconventional, extremes, erratic action, instability, dispensing with nonessentials, separations. Uranus awakens, uproots, interrupts, surprises, challenges, unsettles, reverses, instigates, revolts, resists, invents, uninhibits, separates, develops, evolves.

Neptune

Spiritual or escape urge. Beguiling, relaxing, obscuring, transmuting influence. Chemical energy. Symbol of sacrifice, resignation, compassion, atonement, pity, mystery, intrigue, guile, psychism, occultism, psychic perception, vision and dreams, trance states, passivity, elusiveness, distortion, deception, misconception, evasiveness, fraud, procrastination, transmutation, inspiration, idealism, intuition, non-resistance, great spiritual strength, or moral weakness and tendency to follow a line of least resistance. In a strong character it indicates spiritual guidance and protection. In a weak character it brings out desire to avoid responsibility. Neptune absorbs, masks, deceives, conceals, confuses, entices, beguiles, tempts, dissipates, secretes, distorts, cheats, hypnotizes, deludes, inflates, sublimates, solaces, reveals, inspires, transcends.

Pluto

Destroying or reforming urge. Transforming effect. Atomic energy. symbol of decay, erosion, contamination, infections, fertilizing, leveling, destruction, removing of obstacles, disintegration, obsessions, amalgamations, hidden wealth and power, regeneration and transition, death into new life, release of power, strong will, ruthlessness, dictatorship, large corporations, contests. Pluto explores, erodes, corrodes, purges, explodes, destroys, under mines, obliterates, spoils, despoils, poisons, kidnaps, traps, festers, perverts, unearths, reforms, transforms, regenerates, redeems.

The Sun, Jupiter, Mars, Uranus, and Pluto are activating, projecting, stimulating or positive in polarity.

The Moon, Venus, Saturn, and Neptune are reacting, static, responding, or negative in polarity.

Mercury is neutral, modifying or interpreting, its polarity affected by planets in close aspect to it, not only in the individual horoscope but also in the comparisons.

The influence of any planet can be either beneficial or adverse, constructive or destructive as the definitions given above show. Jupiter, for example, can encourage or increase expression of good qualities or can bring out weakness; it all depends upon the planets aspected. In the case of malefic planets, some combinations of Saturn and Mars, or Saturn and Neptune, or Saturn and Pluto, may have mutually modifying effect, but in most cases conjunctions or bad aspects between the malefics bring out the adverse or destructive sides of the planets involved, unless balanced by good aspects from Venus, Sun, Jupiter, or Mercury.

The square aspect between the benefics does not deny good effects, but simply indicates some difference in the application or expression of the urges represented by these planets which in turn could create misunderstanding or irritation between the individuals.

When interpreting the aspects, in comparisons, the conjunction and opposition tend to stimulate and excite. The sextile and trine blend, harmonize or inspire the good qualities symbolized by the planets forming those aspects. The square hinders or frustrates or will intensify the adverse qualities, creating problems of adjustment and causing either inner tensions in one individual or both, or open conflict between them along the lines indicated by the planets forming the square.

The sextile and trine and some of the conjunctions will offer clues for working out the problems of adjustment indicated by the squares or the testing oppositions.

Regardless of whether favorable or discordant, the conjunction is always the most compelling and significant aspect in its operation; the opposition is next in importance. The square is the most testing and challenging for adjustment; the sextile and trine the most passive though more conducive to ultimate and lasting harmony. The orb of influence between planets in a comparison is ten degrees, although fifteen degrees may be allowed in the case of the Sun.

Chapter 8
Comparison of Aspects

In the following comparisons it is to be understood that the planet in one chart is applying to the planet in the other chart.

Sun

Sun Conjunct Sun (☉☌☉)

Creative power urges combine. Individuals born in the same sign will either be unusually compatible or will irritate each other. It all depends on other aspects in the charts. Should they have many traits in common, it either aids understanding and agreement or will cause the greatest antagonism or rivalry. If there are many common interests the combination can work out very well for most associations. It is probably better if there are a few years difference in age between individuals.

This combination can be favorable for friendships or for parent-child or other family relationships. Whether it is favorable for marriage depends upon the related positions of Sun and Moon, respective Moons and other planetary sign positions and aspects.

I once knew a man and wife born on the same day of the same year, though at different hours and localities. They seemed to be well adjusted. The marriage had lasted for more than five years at the time I met them, and they had two children. This is the only case I ever encountered of a husband and wife being born on the same day and year.

Sun Opposite Sun (☉☍☉)

Creative and power urges either oppose or balance each other. Individuals born in opposite signs sometimes attract, sometimes repel each other. As in the case of the conjunction, it depends on other aspects between the horoscopes.

If one of the Suns has an opposition from Saturn, Neptune, Uranus or Mars, the chances are that harmony will be difficult to achieve, since the Saturn, or whatever the malefic is, would be in conjunction with the other individual's Sun. But testimony can not be given on one point alone. Harmony is usually better with one's own sex when Suns are in opposite signs. In marriage there may be considerable rivalry where Sun opposes Sun. Much compromise may be necessary and the wife generally makes most concessions to the husband. So in the case of Sun opposite Sun, reactions depend on other points in the horoscopes.

Sun Square Sun (⊙□⊙)

Creative and power urges, and individual temperaments can clash. This puts the individuals at cross-purposes, especially if Suns are in fixed signs. Ambition or individual objectives do not adjust easily. It is less conflicting for friendships than for other relationships. In love and marriage it can be frustrating. One individual must do most of the compromising and conciliating and that one usually feels frustrated.

Sun Sextile or Trine Sun (⊙⚹⊙; ⊙△⊙)

Creative and power urges harmonize easily. Temperaments adjust readily. There is mutual sympathy and understanding of ideals and aims. Favorable for any and all relationships, provided the comparisons show no great number of conflicts. Usually good for marriage, especially the sextile.

Sun Conjunct, Sextile or Trine Moon (⊙☌☽; ⊙⚹☽; ⊙△☽)

Creative and power urge blends with the domestic, submissive urge. Masculine and feminine instincts of individuals combine well. Here there is harmony of personality, interchange of sympathy, good mental affinity, and mutual understanding. Personality traits complement each other, yet are not identical. Each possesses something of the other's nature. The Moon individual is intuitive and sensitive in reaction to the Sun individual. The Sun is protective toward the Moon. The conjunction is a powerful attraction between the sexes. It is better if the man's Sun aspects the woman's Moon, but in any case it indicates ability to achieve compatibility and harmony in close association. When the woman's Sun conjuncts the man's Moon she might try to lead or dominate him, which is not so wide, though if she is aware of this tendency she can overcome it.

Sun Opposite Moon (⊙☍☽)

Creative and power urge opposes yet attracts the domestic, submissive urge. Here there is attraction and exchange of emotional feeling, though not quite so congenial as in the case of the conjunction. Much depends upon other aspects in the comparison as to whether the attraction will be lasting or temporary. If lasting, the Sun individual as a rule will be the dominating influence. They can achieve much together. Usually favorable for marriage if other aspects support it.

Sun Square Moon (☉□☽)

Power urge clashes with domestic urge. Here we have some difference of temperament, especially between individuals of the opposite sex. How serious these differences might become depends on other aspects. Where marriage is concerned, the Sun individual may sometimes be inconsiderate, or will ignore or offend the Moon, usually without intending to. The Moon individual will need to guard against being too sensitive and taking trifles too seriously where this relationship is concerned. This aspect is not seriously conflicting, however, as the differences are mostly of temperament, which can be adjusted if the individuals want to achieve harmony together.

Sun Conjunct, Sextile or Trine Mercury (☉☌☿; ☉⚹☿; ☉△☿)

Creative power urge harmonizes with mental urge. Good mental understanding and probably many common interests. Agreement and collaboration are easy to attain. The Sun individual can influence viewpoints of the Mercury individual as well as encourage and stimulate the latter's ideas and intellectual progress. This is a good aspect to find between teacher and pupil, parent and child, employer and employee but is favorable wherever found. Mercury understands Sun and understanding always aids agreement and adjustment.

Sun Opposite Mercury (☉☍☿)

Creative power urge opposes or balances mental urge. There is a mental attraction and stimulation here, although the mutual understanding and interest and ability to come to agreement are not so good as in the conjunction. Some differences of viewpoint may be discovered, but whether these would create serious obstacles to harmony and adjustment depends on other aspects.

Sun Square Mercury (☉□☿)

Creative power urge conflicts with mental urge. Diversified or conflicting interests and ideas, and difficulty in coming to agreements. Mercury individual can be evasive toward Sun individual, or if conciliatory, may be insincere. Sun may be patronizing or will tend to ignore or disregard mental qualities and ideas of Mercury. Both parties are apt to question the judgment of the other, whether they voice their doubt or not.

Sun Conjunct, Sextile, or Trine Venus (☉☌♀, ☉⚹♀,☉△♀)

Creative power urge harmonizes with social or love urge. Here you have a magnetic attraction, especially in the conjunction. These are aspects of sympathy, affection, friendship, companionship, generosity, devotion, loyalty, unselfishness toward each other, mutual admiration, and encouragement. Very good for domestic felicity and fidelity in marriage. Individuals are mutually inspiring and encouraging and co-operative. The convivial and social interests are usually in agreement, thus affording enjoyment of the same pleasures.

Sun Opposite or Square Venus (☉☍♀, ☉□♀)

Power or creative urge conflicts with social or love urge. No aspect between Sun and Venus could be seriously antagonistic. In these combinations there is less complete harmony and sympathy between individuals than in the above series of Sun-Venus aspects. There may be differences of taste, background, or of cultural, social, or recreational inclinations. Where horoscopes of the opposite sex are being considered, the opposition and square may indicate a little envy, jealousy, possessiveness, and extravagance or overindulgence of one partner toward the other. The opposition is a very strong aspect of attraction, however, where love and marriage are concerned, and if other aspects support the combination, it can be favorable for marriage, though the emotional qualifications mentioned above must be taken into account in discussing marital endurability.

Sun Conjunct Mars (☉☌♂)

Creative power urge combines with aggressive urge. This aspect stimulates the aggressive spirit and ambitions of both parties. It can be mutually encouraging, though sometimes arouses rivalry. Progress together will be rapid where the individuals are fully cooperative. Between persons of the opposite sex and especially in marriage, it is best if the wife's Mars applies to the husband's Sun. Where the reverse is found, the man tends to be domineering, demanding and impatient toward the wife, though he will protect and defend her. He will stimulate her independence and power urge, thus sometimes arousing rivalry and resistance in her. It is an aspect of sexual attraction and compatibility.

Sun Sextile or Trine Mars (☉⚹♂; ☉△♂)

Power urge harmonizes with aggressive urge. Each individual stimulates self-confidence, energy, ambition, enthusiasm, initiative, courage, enterprising spirit in the other. In close associations there is usually agreement in working toward a common goal.

Sun Opposite Mars (☉☍♂)

Power urge opposes aggressive urge. Unless there are many harmonious aspects to balance it, this is a very conflicting aspect. The two persons can stimulate each other, but rather too much so. They resist each other and cooperation becomes difficult to achieve. There is likely to be irritation, clashes of temperament and a tendency to quarrel over objectives. There can be jealousy and rivalry between them. They will be impatient with each other and even vindictive. Many harmonious aspects will be needed in any union chart to offset this one.

Sun Square Mars (☉□♂)

Power urge conflicts with aggressive urge. The ambitions of the two individuals will conflict. Their reactions to each other will be emotional and often explosive. Hostility is easily aroused. They "lock horns," as the saying goes. They put each other on the defensive, and this often results in arguments and quarrels. It is a difficult aspect to find in marriage comparisons, for the marriage will endure only if there is a great deal of patience and forbearance. One individual will have to give in to the other in most situations. This often causes in that individual a feeling of rebellion, frustration, and inner resentment. It can affect the health in the one who submits.

Sun Conjunct, Sextile, or Trine Jupiter (☉☌♃, ☉✶♃, ☉△♃)

Creative power urge blends with benevolent, protective urge. This is an inspirational influence, a sign of mutual encouragement, tolerance, helpfulness, forgiveness. There is sympathy, protectiveness, loyalty, generosity, and as a rule mutual trust and confidence. When they try, they can and instinctively will bring out the best in each other. They benefit each other in either or both a spiritual and material way. Regardless of any adverse aspects between the horoscopes where one of these Sun-Jupiter combinations occurs, there will be a desire to protect and help. The one having the Sun aspected by Jupiter will usually drive the greatest benefit from the association in most cases.

Sun Opposite or Square Jupiter (☉☍♃, ☉□♃)

Power urge challenges benevolent urge. These aspects are not actually discordant, but there is a little less amiability and less give-and-take than in the more favorable aspects between Sun and Jupiter. In these combinations the Sun individual may be tempted to shift responsibility to Jupiter. Helpfulness is more one-sided than reciprocal. The Jupiter individual may promise more than he can deliver, although he does assist. In the square there can be conflict between the aspirations, ideals, or ethics of the Jupiter person and the material ambitions of the Sun individual. The Sun expects too much of Jupiter. If the majority of interchart aspects are harmonious, this Sun-Jupiter aspect can be easily resolved; otherwise we must label it doubtful.

Sun Sextile or Trine Saturn (☉✶♄, ☉△♄)

Power urge harmonizes with security urge. These aspects denote a good balancing of the confidence, enthusiasm, ambition, organizational ability, and persistence needed to carry out any mutual purposes. It ensures agreement in the handling of problems, allocation of duties, authority and responsibility. Saturn links stability and loyalty to Sun. It is particularly good for business and financial associations. Any limiting or restraining influence that Saturn might hold on the Sun works mainly for the ultimate good of both. The Sun encourages and stimulates confidence in Saturn. In marriage these aspects aid endurance.

Sun Conjunct Saturn (☉♂♄)

Power urge and security urge combine. This aspect can be good or unfortunate, depending on whether the majority of interchart aspects are harmonious or frictional. Saturn slows Sun, but this could be for the latter's good. Saturn reminds Sun of duties and responsibilities and can be a bit critical. The Sun does much to encourage and vitalize Saturn, alleviate worries, fears, or other negative mental attitudes in Saturn. Sun often has to wait for Saturn who may be slow in some way (or seems so to Sun). Saturn depends on Sun for inspiration; sometimes throws responsibility on Sun or will try to blame Sun for troubles. Saturn can depress or discourage Sun, and may put a damper on his spirits and enthusiasms, but this might help him to be more practical and realistic. Sun will be tolerant and forgiving toward Saturn.

There is loyalty between the individuals if the comparison can be judged a good one. A Sun conjunct Saturn bond is hard to break. Saturn needs the Sun and holds him. Saturn should try not to let Sun feel it is bondage. Saturn has a confining influence on Sun. Sun may learn needed lessons of discipline and patience through Saturn. In marriage a Sun-Saturn conjunction is occasionally found where there is a wide difference of ages, or where the wife is older than the husband. It is better in this aspect if the wife's Sun aspects the husband's Saturn. In nearly all cases Saturn will benefit most from the relationship, as the Sun will have to make most of the concessions and do most of the compromising to ensure harmony.

The Saturn partner should guard against selfishness, criticism, coldness, unresponsiveness, putting too much emphasis on discipline and duty or depreciating the aims of the Sun. Too much Saturn pessimism can wear down the vitality and optimism of Sun. Sometimes Saturn puts too much blame on Sun for things that go wrong. Saturn may be as sympathetic as he or she can be, but is usually loyal and dependable. If there are many good aspects in the comparison, the Sun-Saturn conjunction can prove a stabilizing influence, for the caution of Saturn can restrain any reckless tendency in Sun. But in all cases, Saturn needs to cultivate the "light touch" to make his practical and serious viewpoints acceptable to Sun.

In parent-child relationships where the parent's Saturn aspects the child's Sun, the parent can be too severe and strict, put too much emphasis on duty, or be overly concerned for the child's physical safety, thus building anxiety or fear in the child. The child can develop a fear of the parent which would make the child deceitful and could adversely affect his health.

Sun Opposite Saturn (☉☍♄)

Similar to the conjunction, except that it brings out more resistance between individuals. The limiting, restricting qualities of Saturn are keenly felt by the Sun. Saturn is apt to be demanding and uncompromising and will oppose the Sun needlessly. Sometimes Saturn will be suspicious, condemning, exacting, complaining, critical, or overbearing, or will humiliate Sun.

Sun Square Saturn (☉□♄)

Power urge conflicts with security urge. Here the ideas of security, stability, duty, economy, and responsibility will conflict with the optimism, ambition, and confidence of Sun. Saturn restricts, delays, or frustrates Sun. Saturn will worry, burden, limit, discipline, hinder, discourage or depress Sun, if not in words or action, through the experiences of their association. The pressure of Saturn will be more difficult for the Sun to accept or adjust to than in the case of the other Saturn-Sun aspects. This square often produces setbacks or losses in business, as well as in marriage. Saturn can limit or interfere with Sun in some way, bringing to the latter numerous debts or burdens or problems to be solved. Saturn sometimes disappoints Sun or causes him to become discouraged. It may tear down his hope and confidence. This may not be intentional, but due to experiences or to the disposition of the Saturn individual. The ambitions of Sun are delayed in realization because of problems or responsibilities which Saturn brings into the relationship.

In marriage, Saturn brings or incurs a limitation or obligation which works some hardship on Sun.

Sun Conjunct Uranus (☉☌♅)

Power urge combines with individualism or freedom urge. This aspect can induce a magnetic or romantic, although spasmodic, attraction between individuals of opposite sex. It usually starts as infatuation. Whether fortunate or unfortunate depends on other aspects between the horoscopes. In harmonious charts it stimulates originality, creative power, spiritual ideals, intuitions or new ideas in one or both individuals. Uranus awakens aims and talents in Sun. In discordant charts it tends to excite unconventionalism, rebellion, and explosive reactions of one person toward the other. Whether fortunate or not, there is always something unique in the relationship where this aspect occurs. The individuals are frequently separated by circumstances, such as one having to travel. Uranus is always unpredictable in his reactions to Sun. The Sun individual never is sure how the Uranus person will react in a given situation. To some Sun individuals this might be intriguing or stimulating, while to others it might be disconcerting. In friendships the aspect denotes a sporadic, though interesting and stimulating, association. It is a very good aspect to find between astrologer and client. It is doubtful for business partnerships since the erratic tendency of Uranus makes for shaky foundations or has a disorganizing effect on Sun. Much depends on the nature of the business. For anything creative or artistic it might be very good.

Sun Sextile or Trine Uranus (☉⚹♅, ☉△♅)

Creative urge and individualism blend harmoniously. There is spiritual harmony and usually a mutual benefit from the association. Exchange of ideas stimulates originality in both parties. Intellectual and creative powers are awakened. Such individuals are always interesting to each other. Where romance and marriage are considered, these aspects enliven the romantic feelings and increase mutual interests and companionship.

Sun Opposite or Square Uranus (☉☍♅, ☉□♅)

Creative or power urge conflicts with freedom urge. There is a conflict of individualities in the combination. The unpredictable Uranus keeps the Sun ''up in the air.'' Uranus will resent the influence of Sun and rebel against any authority Sun shows. Cooperation seldom is achieved when either of these aspects occurs between two charts. It often causes separations or a sporadic association. Unless the two persons are poised and self-disciplined, a close association is not likely to be satisfying to either party. The square is the more adverse of the two, sometimes causing violent reactions. Uranus resists Sun and both are impatient and rebellious toward each other.

Sun Conjunct Neptune (☉☌♆)

Power urge combines with escape or atonement urge. When there are a majority of good aspects linking two charts, this aspect in it will indicate a spiritual tie, much inspiration, understanding, sympathy, empathy and unusual sensitivity to each other. There is a psychic tie or stimulus of occult interests between the two. Between persons of opposite sex, the aspect inspires reverence, romance, devotion, idealism, tolerance, and personal sacrifice. Much compassion, and sometimes pity, establish the relationship. The attachment is subtle, but forges a strong bond. However, when the two charts show many discordant aspects, Sun conjunct Neptune, even though inducing sympathy, also produces seductiveness and deception. Neptune may make promises which are not kept. Neptune will always be elusive or unfathomable in some way to the Sun, even where the comparison is considered good.

Sun Sextile or Trine Neptune (☉⚹♆, ☉△♆)

Power urge harmonizes with spiritual urge. These aspects are like favorable sides of the conjunction. There is a strong psychic tie here, too. This aspect aids mutual confidence. There is much attraction and sympathy between the individuals. In friendships, enjoyment of music and aesthetic, occult, or metaphysical interests ensures congeniality.

Sun Opposite or Square Neptune (☉☍♆, ☉□♆)

Power urge clashes with escape or spiritual urge. Neptune will exhibit elusive, evasive, deceptive qualities in reaction toward Sun. Sun is baffled by Neptune. There is lack of trust between individuals. Neptune can be misleading, appearing submissive, but subtly eluding the influence of Sun. The problems or situations provoked by these discordant Sun-Neptune aspects are never quite as bad as they appear, nor as good as envisioned. The square is worse than the opposition. These aspects are difficult in marriage as they breed misunderstanding, doubt, confusion, distrust, deception, and sometimes infidelity in one or both partners.

Sun Conjunct Pluto (☉☌♇)

Power urge combines with reforming or destroying urge. There will be a struggle for authority, especially if both individuals are strong willed. Pluto forces change upon the Sun in close associations, changes of circumstances, or through experiences together; even personality changes can occur. Whether these happen for good or ill depends on other aspects in the comparison. Conflict is threatened when the individuals are not of different generations, as in parent-child relationships, for different generations bring different viewpoint of life.

Pluto can have a hypnotic influence on Sun which is either good or bad depending on the comparison as a whole. The aspect is sometimes found when there is attraction between individuals of widely different cultural or educational backgrounds and sometimes between people of different races.

Sun Sextile or Trine Pluto (☉⚹♇, ☉△♇)

Power urge harmonizes with reforming urge. There is not much reaction here. The aspect can be favorable for the exchange of ideas. It stimulates enterprise and ambition in both individuals. It can be favorable in business or political associations, and is especially good if the individuals are engaged in research or promotional activities.

Sun Opposite or Square Pluto (☉⚯♀, ☉□♀)

Creative urge conflicts with reforming urge. Reactions are frictional if the association is a close one. Pluto resists authority of Sun and will be jealous, rebellious, demanding, and even vindictive. Pluto resists correction from Sun, and will try to change Sun. In marriage, Pluto can undermine the confidence of Sun, and could have an unfortunate influence on Sun's moral or ethical ideas. Even in good charts, Pluto will try to change or reform Sun. The association can produce infidelity in marriage. Unless differences of temperament are understood and adjusted, the reactions of Sun and Pluto in these aspects are adjudged unfavorable. In friendships it indicates occasional tests of tolerance and loyalty.

Moon

For Moon aspects with Sun see pages 50 and 51.

Moon Conjunct Moon (☽☌☽)

Feminine and domestic urges are similar. There is similarity of viewpoint and tendency of mood and disposition. The two individuals will be sensitive to each other's moods and feelings. Reactions often produce telepathic exchange of thought. They agree on little things, and have many likes, dislikes, and tastes in common. There is mutual understanding and sympathy. Many similar traits of personality will be noticed. This aspect aids agreement, adaptability, and cooperation in any type of association.

Moon Sextile or Trine Moon (☽⚹☽, ☽△☽)

These aspects help to establish harmony between individuals, There is sympathy and agreement in little things. Dispositions are congenial. Chances for harmony in any type of association are aided by these aspects.

Moon Opposite Moon (☽⚯☽)

In moods and feelings the two personalities are different, but there is seldom any serious conflict. Dispositions adjust well if the charts are harmonious as a whole. As in the conjunction, there is much sensitivity to each other's moods and feelings. In marriage it can be a very good combination, aiding cooperation and lending a pleasant give-and-take in little everyday affairs. It is generally found to indicate harmony in domestic and family life. It can be judged as an aid to sexual compatibility.

Moon Square Moon (☽□☽)

This can cause a bit of trouble. There is a difference of viewpoint and interest and lack of understanding or patience with each other's moods and feelings; sometimes lack of consideration in little things. There may be misunderstandings unless many good aspects counterbalance this one. In marriage there is a tendency for the wife to exaggerate trivalities, since trifles upset the wife more than the husband as a rule. It is not an aspect which provokes serious friction or problems, but petty irritations which prevent full harmony and cooperation.

Moon Conjunct, Sextile, or Trine Mercury (☽☌☿, ☽⚹☿, ☽△☿)

Feeling and mental perceptions combine with intelligence. These aspects indicate a quick perception of each other's ideas and views. There is a mental affinity and quick perception of each other's mental qualities. The aspects facilitate conversational interchange and good understanding between the two persons. They can promote each other's mental development. Many mutual interests will be encouraged. There often is telepathic thought projection.

Moon Opposite Mercury (☽☍☿)

This aspect also stimulates an interesting exchange of ideas and stimulates mental perception and agility of mental reaction in each other, but without the complete agreement usually found in the conjunction, sextile, or trine. Viewpoints are occasionally at variance, causing minor misunderstandings or difficulty in coming to agreement.

Moon Square Mercury (☽□☿)

The Moon is hypersensitive to the ideas, viewpoints, and feelings of Mercury. Moon will sometimes misinterpret words or gestures of Mercury. Interests and tastes differ in trifling ways. Understanding will not be complete or clear in exchange of ideas. Moon is confused by Mercury's reasoning at times. Mercury can become irritated and impatient if Moon does not immediately grasp his thoughts or if Moon perceives ahead of Him. Mercury takes critical attitude or is tactless in expression of thoughts to Moon. Mercury disregards or fails to understand moods and feelings of Moon. Misunderstandings can occur. This is mildly irritating rather than seriously antagonistic. If harmony and cooperation are sincerely desired by the individuals, good aspects between Sun and Moon, Sun and Mercury, or Moon and Venus can help to resolve misunderstandings indicated by the Moon adverse to Mercury.

Moon Conjunct, Sextile, or Trine Venus (☽☌♀, ☽⚹♀, ☽△♀)

Domestic urges harmonize with social urges. This aspect indicates conviviality and congeniality. Harmony, sympathy, a spirit of consideration for each other, and helpfulness are stimulated by these aspects. There will be deep affection and devotion if other aspects show a growing and lasting attachment to be possible. There is a strong attraction for love and marriage. Individuals in whose charts one of these aspects occurs can have a soothing, calming, encouraging effect on each other. They can benefit each other through service, and often in material or financial ways. They have many tastes and interests in common, which aid companionship and enjoying social engagements together. These aspects will do much to mitigate mental or personality conflicts between two persons, if any exist.

Moon Opposite Venus (☽☍♀)

This is almost as favorable as the above. It is a strong attraction where love and marriage are considered, second in importance to the conjunction of Moon and Venus. Much affection is shown between the individuals. In the opposition there may be fewer mutual interests as in the case of the conjunction, sextile, or trine.

Moon Square Venus (☽□♀)

This is not harmfully discordant, but not so favorable as other Moon-Venus aspects. In the square there may be petty jealousy of one individual toward the other and in close relationships, minor domestic discords. Some differences of tastes or social-reactional inclinations are indicated. Adjustment will be easy if there is sincere affection between the two individuals.

Moon Conjunct Mars (☽☌♂)

Mars stimulates the mind and imagination of Moon. Emotions of Moon will be easily aroused by Mars. Sometimes the Moon will be hypersensitive in reactions to Mars. Mars will want to lead the Moon, will try to take command, or coerce. Between persons of the opposite sex the aspect may stimulate physical attraction. It is one of the strong attractions that lead to love and marriage if other aspects support the possibility. It is best if the man's Mars aspects the woman's Moon. This aspect stimulates the propagative instincts and encourages conception. If the woman's Mars is on the man's Moon, she may try to dominate the man in the home or may often be impatient, argumentative, or tactless with him. Sometimes she will be too demanding and may nag.

Moon Sextile or Trine Mars (☽⚹♂, ☽△♂)

Mars stimulates imagination, ideas, and self-confidence in Moon. In home and family environment it aids cooperation and efficiency in getting things done together. In marriage the aspect of the husband's Mars to the wife's Moon encourages reproduction.

Moon Opposite or Square Mars (☽☍♂, ☽□♂)

Mars can be highly irritating to Moon. Mars' actions can upset poise and disposition of Moon. These aspects produce serious personality conflicts. In the opposition, where love and marriage are concerned, there may be a strong attraction, but equally strong emotional reactions of a discordant nature. These aspects can precipitate indiscretions. If the woman's Mars applies to the man's Moon, she will tend to nag. Mars will be rude or abrupt toward Moon. Moon is hypersensitive in reactions to Mars.

Moon Conjunct, Sextile, or Trine Jupiter (☽☌♃, ☽✶♃, ☽△♃)

These are unusually good aspects. They encourage mutual confidence and respect. Jupiter stimulates imagination, ideas, and self-confidence in Moon. Jupiter lends assistance to Moon, and will be patient, tolerant, protective, and generous. If the association is not an especially happy one, Jupiter will never hold any lasting ill-will toward Moon. Moon usually has favors granted when she appeals to Jupiter. In the conjunction, Jupiter is especially protective, generous and helpful, but can be too indulgent as well. Moon will be generally adaptable and cooperative. In marriage, these aspects stimulate fertility, assuming the health and age of the wife is conducive to child bearing. If Jupiter is religious or spiritually inclined, he can have a very inspiring and enabling effect on Moon, bringing out the best facets of Moon's personality.

Moon Opposite or Square Jupiter (☽☍♃, ☽□♃)

These aspects are not actually hostile, but not as completely favorable as above. Moon overestimates promises of Jupiter, thus expecting too much and laying himself open to little disappointments. Also, Moon may be tempted to take advantage of Jupiter's benevolence and can demand too much. Jupiter, however, sometimes imposes on Moon. The square, in marriage, may denote religious, family or in-law problems which, although not serious, can be emotionally disturbing.

Moon Conjunct Saturn (☽☌♄)

Whether this aspect works for good or ill depends on other aspects between the charts. Saturn tends to discipline Moon. This factor may be stabilizing in many cases, but in others Saturn may have a depressing and limiting effect on Moon. Saturn can affect the moods and feelings of Moon adversely; he also can be critical of Moon. A tendency to be cool, indifferent, or demanding may show up. Where there is agreement of aims between the two persons, the aspect aids the practical application of abilities, since Saturn can help the Moon to plan and build, and

Moon can be adaptable. Saturn will need to avoid selfishness toward Moon. Saturn looks to Moon for understanding and sympathy. If Moon inclines to pessimism, Saturn will make him moreso, and also can further discourage Moon. Saturn brings burden, worry, duty, responsibility, or anxiety to Moon.

Where marriage is concerned, Saturn can give Moon a sense of security unless the Saturn individual himself is insecure. Saturn is protective toward Moon. This aspect makes an attachment very binding as a rule, whether for friendship, business, or marriage. It is sometimes found in horoscopes of persons of widely different ages.

Moon Sextile or Trine Saturn (☽✶♄, ☽△♄)

Saturn steadies Moon and Moon enlarges the ideas of Saturn. Emotions of Moon are stabilized by Saturn. Saturn will be dependable and steadfast toward Moon. It can counsel Moon, for there is usually mutual respect. These aspects encourage friendly contacts between persons of wide difference in ages. It can be considered a good aspect in horoscopes of child and parent. Saturn brings out conservative qualities in Moon. It is a good aspect in any association of a dependent or underling to one in authority, such as student-teacher, employee-employer. It is good, also, for any business association. In marriage this aspect furthers domestic tranquility, order in the home and agreement in regard to management of money. Parents with this aspect usually are able to agree about training of children.

Moon Opposite Saturn (☽☍♄)

This aspect tends to weaken sympathy between two individuals. Saturn disciplines Moon and the latter may resent it. Saturn can be unjust, critical, unkind, inconsiderate, or selfish toward Moon. Saturn will oppose more readily than agree with Moon. Saturn arouses worry, discouragement, or some other negative attitude in Moon which may become difficult for Moon to throw off. Saturn disregards moods and feelings of Moon, who becomes more sensitive in reaction as time goes on unless an inner defense is built. Between members of a family or in marriage, Saturn may place too much responsibility on Moon, blame him for troubles, or limit him in some way.

Saturn demands much attention from Moon and is hard to please. This tries the patience of Moon. Moon will have to learn patience and forbearance in this association. In marriage there may be domestic difficulties and financial disagreements, or troubles which threaten marital harmony with other members of the family.

Moon Square Saturn (☽□♄)

This is similar to the opposition but more inclined to produce conflict.

Saturn discourages, limits, frustrates, and delays the efforts and progress of Moon, disregarding his feelings. The duties and responsibilities of Saturn will discourage or depress Moon. Unless there are many good aspects between the two charts to balance this one, the individuals will not be of much benefit to each other. Saturn will derive the most benefit. It is not good for marriage, especially if the man's Saturn aspects the woman's Moon. If the woman's Saturn aspects the man's Moon she will tend to nag and will be too critical, exaggerating trifles. This can be a source of misunderstanding and disagreement. Sometimes in-laws will prove a source of trouble between two persons where this aspect is found.

Moon Conjunct Uranus (☽♂♅)

This excites mutual interest and is intellectually stimulating. Sometimes the unpredictable Uranus proves irritating to Moon, especially if Moon likes order and system. Between persons of opposite sex the aspect can indicate a spontaneous and magnetic attraction and sometimes an unconventional one. It arouses romantic feelings, but unless there are many aspects to bind the individuals, they may be changeable or fickle toward each other. It has the suggestion of infatuation or fascination that will be temporary, but if the association can become permanent, this aspect stimulates a continuing romantic appeal. In friendship the association is apt to be spasmodic or sporadic. Attachments may not be lasting unless other aspects indicate it. Uranus qualities can upset Moon's emotional pose if Moon is extremely sensitive. In marriage it can indicate many changes of residence, some of which might be disturbing to the Moon personality.

Moon Sextile or Trine Uranus (☽⚹♅, ☽△♅)

Uranus awakens and inspires ideas in Moon. Moon's imagination can stimulate the originality and versatility of Uranus. The relationship always has something unusual in it. Uranus assists Moon in unusual or unexpected ways.

Moon Opposite or Square Uranus (☽☍♅, ☽□♅)

This aspect can arouse irritations between two persons. Uranus appears very changeable and unpredictable, which confuses Moon, disturbing his moods and emotions. Uranus tends to disregard or is inconsiderate of Moon. Any romantic attraction where this aspect occurs can lead to an unconventional or indiscreet relationship unless individuals are very high-minded and able to resist such temptations. Uranus stimulates ideas in Moon but tests Moon's adaptability. Associations may not last long unless other interchart aspects indicate a permanent association. If this is the case, this Moon-Uranus aspect will indicate numerous separations, changes in domestic affairs, or many moves made which are not always acceptable to Moon. In marriage, individual career aims can be a source of friction, especially if the woman's Uranus is aspecting the man's Moon.

Moon Conjunct, Sextile, or Trine Neptune (☽♂♆, ☽✶♆, ☽△♆)

This aspect indicates a psychic tie. The individuals are unusually sensitive to each other's moods and feelings. There is often telepathic communication. There is much sympathy between them. Neptune may seem a bit aloof to Moon at times, especially in the conjunction. Any of these aspects can indicate much mutual inspiration, and in high-type individuals, spiritual accord and mutual devotion. The sextile and trine are not as strong as the conjunction, but do assist compatibility. There is much mutual sympathy, consolation, and comfort. Any interest in mysticism or occult study in either person will be brought out and increased by this aspect.

Moon Opposite or Square Neptune (☽☍♆, ☽□♆)

There is too much sensitivity to each other's moods and feelings, making the reaction overly emotional and a little disturbing. Neptune can bring confusion and perplexity of mind to Moon. He sometimes precipitates misunderstandings which cannot be clarified. Neptune always seems a bit of a mystery to Moon, and in some cases the Moon person will suspect trickery. If both individuals are weak-willed and given to dissolute habits, they will have an unfortunate influence on each other. Neptune can be deceptive to Moon and can cause the latter much concern or even trouble. It is not a good aspect to find in marriage charts.

Moon Conjunct Pluto (☽♂♀)

Either very good or very bad, depending on other aspects. Pluto enlarges conceptions and ideas and stimulates imagination in Moon, but also can arouse fears or vague repulsions of Moon toward him. Pluto is absorbing and possessive, sometimes given to jealousy. He may try to dominate Moon and change and reform something in his nature. Between the sexes it is a testimony of physical attraction.

Moon Sextile or Trine Pluto (☽✶♀, ☽△♀)

Some mutual benefit, but this is not a very strong aspect. It can be good in a business, political, or professional association. It would be especially good if the individuals were engaged in any form of research work or group activities.

Moon Square or Opposite Pluto (☽□♀, ☽☍♀)

Pluto has a disrupting influence on Moon. The aspect tends to create antipathy rather than agreement. Pluto will seem contrary to Moon and his influence to Moon can be in some way unfortunate. In marriage there may be serious misunderstandings which cause domestic and family troubles. Problems with a sexual origin also could arise.

Mercury

For Mercury aspects with Sun and Moon see pages 51 and 59.

Mercury Conjunct Mercury (☿σ☿)

This is a very good aspect to find between two charts since it indicates similarity of mental ideas and reasoning processes. It fosters understanding and agreement. Good intellectual stimulation is augured, even where individuals have different educational backgrounds. Two individuals will find much to discuss and will agree in principle at least. The two minds learn much from each other. The aspect stimulates conversational give-and-take, which enlivens the association.

Mercury Sextile or Trine Mercury (☿⚹☿, ☿△☿)

This aspect also indicates harmony and agreement on the mental level. It abets understanding. Any difference of opinion can be easily resolved, adjusted, or reconciled. Many mutual interests are discovered. These aspects encourage mental development in each and stimulate ideas and conversational facility between individuals. The two persons can learn much together and from each other.

Mercury Opposite Mercury (☿☍☿)

Differences of viewpoint may occur, but there can be a stimulating give-and-take which proves mentally inspiring. It is not altogether conflicting unless Mercury is found in fixed signs, which would indicate obstinacy in viewpoints that can cause difficulty in arriving at agreements.

Mercury Square Mercury (☿□☿)

This can cause misunderstandings and serious differences of opinion. There is much criticism of each other. The respective interests go in different directions with not much intellectual inspiration or encouragement between them. It is a difficult aspect to work with in marriage, for it does not promote companionship. Discussions end in an impasse, neither one being able to understand or appreciate the ideas and judgements of the other. It often causes confusion of minds in reaction to each other and can lead to arguments, misunderstanding (or just no understanding), and atmospheric tension in close association. When Mercuries are in fixed signs, stubbornness, which precludes compromise, is added.

Mercury Conjunct, Sextile, or Trine Venus (☿☌♀, ☿✶♀, ☿△♀)

Mutually benefiting. This aspect brings out the best in intellectual, artistic, or cultural interests in both individuals. Many mutual interests consolidate friendships of any close association. It is very good in marriage or in parent-child charts. Mutual understanding through sympathy and affection are ensured. Mercury understands and is considerate of the emotions of Venus. Mutual encouragement of respective aptitudes and talents is indicated. In marriage, the aspect aids cooperation in financial management.

Mercury Opposite or Square Venus (☿☍♀, ☿□♀)

These aspects are not seriously conflicting, nor are they completely harmonious or mutually beneficial as the above. There may be minor irritations in the square at times, especially in a close association. Mercury here tends to disregard the emotional needs or attitudes of Venus and seems cold and calculating to the latter in some way.

Mercury Conjunct Mars (☿☌♂)

Mars stimulates the mental awareness, ideas and self-expression of Mercury, but sometimes causes little irritations, especially if the Mars individual inclines to be headstrong, impatient, or argumentative. Mercury's tendency to reason irritates Mars' urge for immediate action. This aspect may be favorable in some ways, though annoying at times, but if horoscopes show individuals to be adaptable and able to adjust to each other, this Mercury-Mars aspect can be enlivening. It quickens mental ability in Mercury.

Mercury Sextile or Trine Mars (☿✶♂, ☿△♂)

This has all the enlivening and mentally stimulating qualities of the conjunction without the danger of irritation. It brings a promise of mutual interest, mutual helpfulness, and mutual encouragement in any association. Mars inspires self-expression and an increase of learning in Mercury. Mercury encourages the best in Mars' ambitions, and can often suggest application of Mars energy for the latter's advantage.

Mercury Opposite or Square Mars (☿☍♂, ☿□♂)

Here there is a conflict between the aims and aggressive spirit of Mars and the reasoning tendency of Mercury. These aspects can cause misunderstandings, arguments, quarrels, and even more serious friction between two individuals. Cooperation will be difficult to achieve. The square is the most frictional. Mars qualities prove irritating and disturbing to Mercury, though there may be stimulus to thinking. But it stirs up quick temper or tactless speech in Mercury unless he is self controlled.

Mercury Conjunct, Sextile or Trine Jupiter (☿☌♃, ☿✶♃, ☿△♃)

Mutually inspirational. The optimistic, aspirational qualities of Jupiter inspire and bring out the urge for mental advancement in the Mercury individual. A good combination for collaboration along lines of creative self-expression. It is very good in partnerships, including parent-child, teacher-student, or in business or marriage. Mercury's reason keeps the ideals and expansive visions of Jupiter down to earth. Jupiter inspires intellectual, moral, spiritual, and ethical qualities in Mercury. Jupiter is tolerant of the ideas of Mercury and will protect, inspire, and encourage interest in higher education. There is general good will toward each other, and stimulus of wit and humor in either or both individuals.

Mercury Opposite or Square Jupiter (☿☍♃, ☿□♃)

Similar to the above, but not mutually beneficial. Mercury benefits most from the association. Jupiter may promise more than he is able to fulfill. There may be differences of opinion along ethical or religious lines that could be irritating in a close relationship. Mercury will often seem petty to Jupiter. Respective interests will not always coincide. It is not a serious conflict if other aspects in the comparison indicate compatibility.

Mercury Conjunct Saturn (☿☌♄)

Saturn's effect on Mercury is much stronger than Mercury's on Saturn. Mercury can learn much from Saturn, assuming that Saturn is the older or more experienced of the two and has the knowledge and wisdom to offer. Saturn can prove discouraging, disparaging, or too critical of Mercury's ideas, reasoning, judgment, or mental accomplishments. Saturn can cause Mercury to feel inadequate or ineffectual in some way. Saturn will hold Mercury to promises and cause him to feel the pressure of any responsibility that could exist in their relationship. Saturn can restrict Mercury's urge for learning, education, or self-expression, or if he approves, will be very critical and watchful of Mercury's progress. Saturn will tend to nag at times. Mercury can encourage Saturn and talk him out of negative attitudes or worry, and also can encourage progressiveness in Saturn. If Mercury is the older of the two, he will have to answer many questions the Saturn individual asks. Saturn would be resentful of Mercury in some way or other.

Mercury Sextile or Trine Saturn (☿✶♄, ☿△♄)

Saturn stabilizes the mind of Mercury and suggests rather than criticizes. Mercury can appreciate the knowledge and experience of Saturn and can give Saturn new ideas. This is a particularly favorable aspect if found in charts of teacher-student, employer-employee, parent-child, or in business associations.

Mercury Opposite or Square Saturn (☿☍♄, ☿□♄)

Saturn here is very critical, exacting, disapproving, discouraging, and apt to judge harshly or to belittle the mental attainments and ideas of Mercury. Saturn also can bring Mercury worry or limitation of some nature. Saturn can detract from self-confidence of Mercury, and cause resentments to grow in the mind of Mercury unless he can protect himself spiritually. Cooperation is difficult in any association where this occurs unless there are many good aspects to offset it. Many of the Mercury aims meet with delay in realization due to obstacles that Saturn may put in the latter's path. Mercury will seem irritating and careless to Saturn at times. Saturn presents a challenge to Mercury, which can help the latter's growth.

Mercury Conjunct, Sextile, or Trine Uranus (☿☌♅, ☿⚹♅, ☿△♅)

Uranus stimulates and awakens the mind of Mercury and gives him many ideas. Mercury can learn from the association. He helps Uranus bring original conceptions down to the level of practical application. There also can be much intuition between two persons having one of these aspects in the comparison. It heightens enjoyment of each other; especially in the exchange of ideas and conversation. Uranus also can stimulate Mercury's interests along occult or spiritual lines. It is good in an astrologer-client relationship.

Mercury Opposite or Square Uranus (☿☍♅, ☿□♅)

Uranus is stimulating, but also may prove irritating and upsetting to Mercury. The latter may not wish to accept ideas of Uranus. Uranus seems unstable or erratic to Mercury. Mercury seems elusive and superficial to Uranus. These aspects cause some confusion of mind between two individuals. Understanding and adjustment to each other is difficult to achieve. They are apt to be impatient with each other. Much depends upon the general temperament of the individuals, but as a rule these aspects cause considerable friction, especially if the association is close. In the opposition, circumstances bring about many separations and spasmodic trends in the association. In the square there may be much disagreement on little issues that cause irritation. Mercury finds it hard to understand and count on Uranus and is therefore made nervous and upset by the latter. In fact, Uranus usually upsets the nervous system of Mercury in these adverse aspects if the association is a continuous or close one.

Mercury Sextile or Trine Neptune (☿⚹♆, ☿△♆)

Neptune inspires, elevates, and encourages ideas in Mercury. Mutual interests can be discovered for there is a psychic tie in many cases. These aspects establish much mental understanding and telepathic communication. Mercury often can suggest practical expression for the intuition, imagination, or sympathetic urges of Neptune.

Mercury Conjunct Neptune (☿☌♆)

This aspect is similar to the above, but in some cases, Neptune may confuse Mercury or seem evasive or deceptive. Much depends on other aspects in the charts as to whether this one is mutually beneficial or would cause misunderstanding and trouble. There is often a strong telepathic tie. Neptune could have a subtle and adverse influence on Mercury if the former tends to dissipation and the Mercury individual is weak and easily influenced.

Mercury Opposite or Square Neptune (☿☍♆, ☿□♆)

There are misunderstandings or, possibly, deceptions on the part of the Neptune individual. Secrets in his life might not be told to the Mercury individual. In some way a deception is practiced; the two may lie to each other, or one will prove untruthful to the other. Mercury fails to understand or interpret correctly many issues of the association with Neptune. Neptune often seems detached or aloof to Mercury. Mercury is more affected by Neptune than vice versa. In business, fraud could be practiced by one or both.

Mercury in Any Aspect to Pluto

Experiences two individuals have together will stimulate the mind of the Mercury individual and bring changes in both their lives. Much contact together will broaden the viewpoints or expand the range of interests, especially in the Mercury individual. Whether the association contributes to harmony or to the spiritual, mental, or material welfare of the individuals depends upon other factors in the comparison. Pluto's influence on Mercury is stronger than Mercury's on Pluto. Pluto may try to dominate the mind of Mercury, and if so could be ruthless.

Venus

For Venus aspects with Sun, Moon, Mercury see pages 51, 52, 59, 60, and 66.

Venus Conjunct, Sextile or Trine Venus (♀☌♀, ♀✶♀, ✶△♀)

There are many mutual interests, inclinations, and similar attitudes in love, friendship, social life, and affections. In the conjunction the individuals express affection in the same way. These aspects increase congeniality, companionship, conviviality, appreciation of each other, the desire to help each other and an ability to enjoy the same pleasures.

They are sympathetic toward each other and will encourage each other. These aspects are favorable in any type of comparison and can do much to smooth out rough places caused by adverse aspects.

Venus Opposite or Square Venus (♀☍♀, ♀□♀)

Minor discords are indicated, although not seriously conflicting unless many adverse aspects are found between two charts. These Venus aspects indicate minor differences of taste, moral sentiment, and attitude toward social life, beauty, and culture. Affection is not expressed in the same way, and so it is a bit difficult in marriage. There can be differences of opinion on economic management and difficulty in coming to agreement in financial matters.

Venus Conjunct Mars (♀☌♂)

The desire nature of Mars stimulates the love nature of Venus. This is a strong aspect of attraction between the sexes. There is much appeal to emotions. Mars sometimes tends to be possessive, jealous, or impetuous in this association. Venus has a soothing effect on Mars. A good aspect to find in love and marriage if other aspects support it. In romance there could be a temptation to indiscretions before marriage.

Venus Sextile or Trine Mars (♀✶♂, ♀△♂)

Like the conjunction, but without the tendency to emotional excesses, jealousy, or impetuousness. It is a very favorable aspect to be found in the charts of marriage partners.

Venus Opposite or Square Mars (♀☍♂, ♀□♂)

Similar to the conjunction, but with more disturbing emotional reactions. Venus finds Mars too impatient. Sometimes one of the individuals will resist the other and the attraction is not always felt by both. A little too much emotion in this combination can lead to friction and disputes in close association. In love and marriage, jealousy will often raise its head. Unless many harmonious aspects balance these, there will be considerable tension or conflict in love and marriage relationships. In undeveloped types, one or both may be unfaithful to the other.

Venus Conjunct, Sextile, Trine, or Opposite Jupiter (♀☌♃, ♀✶♃, ♀△♃, ♀☍♃)

All aspects here denote mutual help and mutual benefit. Individuals enjoy the same pastimes and cultural activities. The aspect stimulates optimism, self-confidence, good health in both. There is mutual consideration, sympathy, encouragement. It is conducive to development along artistic, ethical, or spiritual lines in either or both. The individuals are generous toward each other. Sometimes the conjunction or opposition stimulates an extravagant streak in one or both, or a tendency to wastefulness or overindulgence, or there may be too much emphasis on social form, appearances, clothes, and material possessions.

Venus Square Jupiter (♀□♃)

There are differences of taste. The individuals can overdo tact, courtesy, and manners toward each other, creating some irritation. It is not actually harmful, but makes for a bit of boredom. They are not completely sincere or frank with each other. Also, there are differences of opinion in the handling of finances.

Venus Conjunct Saturn (♀☌♄)

Saturn stabilizes the emotions of Venus, but can be selfish or jealous. Venus can raise the confidence of Saturn through sympathy and affection. The aspect encourages loyalty, but Saturn must guard against being too insistent on attention. In love and marriage the Saturn individual can chill affections of Venus unless other aspects show much warm response on both sides. Saturn makes marriage binding. Saturn feels much responsibility for Venus, sometimes is over-solicitous of Venus welfare. Saturn will be critical. If criticism is voiced too constantly, Venus will be offended. If criticism is not expressed, Saturn suffers inwardly. This is a good aspect for building financial stability if Venus will heed Saturn, and if they will work together. Saturn feeds on affections that Venus has to offer and can be too intense and demanding in reaction to Venus. The Venus individual can be depressed or restricted at times by Saturn. This aspect increases loyalty and mutual dependence in love and marriage and if other aspects are favorable, this one can be very good. It is an aspect which supports endurability.

Venus Sextile or Trine Saturn (♀✶♄, ♀△♄)

This is similar to the conjunction without the danger of the negative side being brought out, or the demanding and absorbing tendency of Saturn coming into the association.

Venus Opposite or Square Saturn (♀☍♄, ♀□♄)

Venus will have many unhappy experiences through this aspect. Saturn will prove to be demanding, restricting, selfish, condemning, resentful, critical, disapproving, and jealous, and may even dislike Venus. Venus would find it difficult to give affection to Saturn, or if he or she does, it would be mere show inspired by fear or anxiety. This is an unfavorable aspect when found in charts of parent-child, especially if parent has the Saturn. In any close association Saturn brings sorrow or worry to Venus and the latter will usually seek to escape in some way if possible. In love or marriage charts the Venus individual will usually be made unhappy and feel dominated or frustrated. Many economic problems also are likely to be encountered. Saturn tends to impose too much responsibility on Venus; often blames Venus for troubles encountered together. Some Saturn quality or habit may disgust Venus if Venus is very fastidious.

Venus Conjunct Uranus (♀☌♅)

This is a stimulating aspect. It can be good for artistic development if either has artistic or creative talent. It stimulates creative ability and originality of ideas in Venus especially. Many social interests encourage companionship. Uranus has altruistic feelings toward Venus and is tolerant and encouraging. Between persons of opposite sex this aspect excites emotion and arouses romantic feelings. It is a very magnetic attraction. Romance usually starts as an infatuation. There will be something unusual or unconventional in this association. Unless there are many aspects to indicate loyalty and steadfastness, however, the romance may be short-lived. It will be erratic, spasmodic, or changeable. If marriage results, fascination and romance survive and it makes for mutual companionship and much happiness.

Venus Sextile or Trine Uranus (♀⚹♅, ♀△♅)

This also encourage creative expression in both as well as social enjoyment, conviviality, and romance. The individuals can inspire and benefit each other in various ways. It is good in any association.

Venus Opposite or Square Uranus (♀☍♅, ♀□♅)

These aspects are stimulating, but Uranus seems uncertain, unpredictable, and undependable to Venus. Though exciting and interesting, romance can be disappointing or even unfortunate, especially in the case of the square. Individuals may be fickle toward each other and cannot depend on each other. There may be changes of heart, disappointments for both, and separations. Unless there are many good aspects to balance this, it is not recommended for marriage.

Venus Conjunct Neptune (♀☌♆)

Encourages any mutual interests of a cultural type, especially music, drama, dancing, poetry, and art. Love of nature is also enjoyed together. There will be much sympathy between the individuals and in many cases the aspect aids understanding and can create a deep affection and devotion. Neptune will be sympathetic and sacrificing toward Venus, though also elusive and sometimes deceptive. Much depends on other aspects in judging if this one is entirely good. Neptune tends to entice or bewitch Venus. If either or both individuals incline to self-indulgences this aspect will encourage such weaknesses in them. Between individuals of the opposite sex it introduces a note of pity into the attraction. Pity is akin to love, but not always a fortunate beginning for true devotion. There is an unconventional aspect to romance. This planetary combination sometimes produces unlegalized unions. The Venus individual must not lose sight of practical issues of life if marriage is under consideration. This aspect can help to make a marriage ideal—or it could produce disillusionment, and an association which proves disorganizing to the individuals. It all depends upon how mature and responsible the individuals are. If other aspects indicate high endurability this one can be considered favorable.

Venus Sextile or Trine Neptune (♀⚹♆, ♀△♆)

There is mutual sympathy, generosity, kindness, consideration, and a quiet affection and devotion. Many mutual interests stimulated, especially along lines of art, music, dancing, drama, poetry, and photography. Occult interests, or a love of nature, also would be brought out if latent in the individuals. They may, in fact, be the cause of attraction.

Venus Opposite or Square Neptune (♀☍♆, ♀□♆)

There may be attraction between two individuals, or sometimes a one-sided attraction. Much sympathy and compassion is aroused, but there is also likely to be a certain amount of confusion, deception, even evasion on the part of one or both. Venus would be wise to make Neptune prove all he or she says about himself before submitting to a close association. It is an adverse aspect for business or financial associations, as there can be misconceptions and misunderstandings, or deceptions or fraud. Usually, the Venus individual gets the worst end of it. regardless of the respective integrity of the individuals. Neptune in these aspects can be disturbing to Venus affections. Neptune can mislead or deceive, entice, or confuse Venus, even though his intentions may be honorable. In friendships, Neptune will be elusive or deceitful and undependable in some way or simply uncooperative. One or both are insincere toward the other. Sometimes associations with these aspects just drift apart rather than break up through any decisive action or for any special cause. In horoscopes of marriage partners there may be infidelity on the part of one or both partners.

Venus Conjunct, Sextile, or Trine Pluto (♀☌♇, ♀⚹♇, ♀△♇)

The Pluto individual is apt to be demanding, jealous, absorbing, and possessive toward Venus. The sextile and trine are somewhat favorable. Mutual benefits can be realized through the association in an economic or social way. In the conjunction, reconstruction of values is brought about by the association. In close association, such as marriage or business, great difficulty of a financial nature which would lead to antagonism, misrepresentation, and imposition, with Venus getting the worst end of the bargain. In romance, Pluto could have a degrading effect upon Venus, either due to vulgarity or sexual demands. Other aspects must be considered to determine whether the Venus-Pluto conjunction is a mild or serious test to the moral nature of the individuals.

Venus Square or Opposite Pluto (♀□♇, ♀☍♇)

These aspects are generally adverse, especially the square. Pluto would be jealous, possessive, demanding, absorbing, or imposing in some way on Venus. The association would upset the emotions of Venus. In romance and marriage the aspect indicates problems of adjustment, sometimes in sexual relations. Unless the two individuals are on a high spiritual level, one could have a demoralizing influence upon the other. The moral integrity of Venus could suffer. These aspects sometimes indicate differences in social-recreational interests which create discord between the individuals. In romance the aspects sometimes occur in cases of unrequited love. The opposition forces reconstruction of values upon one of both.

Mars

For Mars aspects to Sun, Moon, Mercury, Venus see pages 52, 53, 60, 61, 66, and 70.

Mars Conjunct Mars (♂♂♂)

The quality of energy is similar; desires are often similar or will be in agreement. The tendency of action in two individuals will be similar. If horoscopes show harmony in disposition this aspect can be very good; otherwise it threatens to cause irritation, impatience, anger, and rivalry, since both may want to take the initiative in situations. It is good if the individuals will cooperate.

Mars Sextile or Trine Mars (♂⚹♂, ♂△♂)

Unity of desire, energy, action. The individuals can cooperate effectively. They stimulate each other's courage and ambition. These aspects are helpful in marriage for sexual compatibility and very good in business associations.

Mars Opposite or Square Mars (♂☍♂, ♂□♂)

There is some of conflict of individual wills and desires, subtle if not openly expressed. There is a tendency at times to interfere with or obstruct each other's work. Disputes arise when differences cannot be adjusted. Much depends on other aspects, of course. There is usually some friction or hostility and in the square, vindictiveness is aroused unless individuals are in command of their emotional natures. These Mars aspect do not bring out the best in individual dispositions, so one or both must use much self-control to adjust this. These are very difficult aspects to work with in a close association unless there is much mutual tolerance as shown by other aspects. In marriage they can cause tensions, since the desire natures conflict; or, if they are in agreement, the individuals will not want what they want at the same time. In business or work association there will be differences in technical methods. Cooperation is difficult to achieve. It comes usually at the cost of one submitting to the other, in which case the one submitting will have to fight inner resentments.

Mars Conjunct, Sextile, or Trine Jupiter (♂☌♃, ♂✶♃, ♂△♃)

These aspects stimulate aspirations and ambitions in the individuals. They complement each other, one adding aggressive spirit to the ambitions and aspirations of the other. The aspects stimulate mutual helpfulness in achieving prosperity, but in the case of the conjunction also can stimulate extravagance or, in one or both, a tendency to speculate unwisely. One individual encourages daring in the other, and in many cases, they encourage it in each other. These aspects promote optimism, ambition, and desire for expansion. They are especially favorable when found in charts of business or marriage partners. In some cases, a mutual interest along lines of sports, or love of nature and outdoor recreation will consolidate friendships and aid congeniality in the association.

Mars Opposite or Square Jupiter (♂☍♃, ♂□♃)

These aspects create discord rather than harmony. The respective ambitions conflict. There is apt to be rivalry between them, or one individual will drive the other against his best judgement. There are differences of opinion on ethical or moral points in some cases. There is a tendency to be impatient and to demand too much of each other. Sometimes one promises more than he can fulfill. In business, these aspects encourage foolhardy risks. They are a detriment from an economic standpoint in marriage or business comparisons. These aspects must be stabilized by many good ones if the association is to benefit the individuals. They must respect each other's judgment and strive for careful planning and administration of their affairs or the association will prove unfortunate for economic security. These aspects tend to bring out any trait of extravagance, or wastefulness, or foolhardiness in the nature of either or both parties.

Mars Conjunct Saturn (♂☌♄)

This aspect can be good in many cases; it depends on other aspects in the comparison. Mars stimulates ambition and progressive instinct in Saturn. Saturn caution restrains the Mars tendency to act too quickly, impulsively, or with sufficient forethought or preparation. If the positive and best sides of these two planets are expressed in this association, this aspect induces cooperation and working for a common goal. It is very good for business associations where the objective is material profit. Saturn always teaches a lesson or puts a brake upon the personal expression denoted by any planet it aspects by conjunction. In this case, Saturn in some ways restricts or limits the activities of Mars, and the latter may have to set aside many personal aims or projects, temporarily if not permanently, or as long as the association lasts. Mars can be irritating to the cautious, practical Saturn, since Mars wants action speedily and hates to wait for results. Saturn puts much responsibility upon Mars and, if Mars is equal to it, it brings out the progressive and enterprising instincts. It can prove a challenge which helps Mars to progress and succeed. Mars stimulates self-confidence in Saturn and thus helps Saturn to resist discouragement and build greater security for himself. Mars rises to emergencies, helping Saturn solve many problems. Mars often may have to wait for the slower Saturn, trying his patience or giving Mars an occasional period of anxiety. In marriage the aspect is a point in favor of endurance. Saturn always binds.

The aspect is difficult in a parent-child relationship, especially if the parent's Saturn falls on the child's Mars. Saturn can be overly severe and critical, and will fail to take into account the child's need for activity and to learn many things by trial and error. Saturn can be too strict in management and too severe in methods of punishment. Also, Saturn can be too anxious for the safety of Mars. If the parent's Mars is on the child's Saturn, there will be impatience with the child who may be slow in some way, and the child can become resentful or even afraid of the parent. Much, of course, depends upon other aspects. If there is love and affection, the aspect can be resolved and work for the good of the child.

Mars Sextile or Trine Saturn (♂⚹♄, ♂△♄)

The courage, ambition, and physical drive of Mars combines well with the caution and carefulness of Saturn. These aspects are favorable for practical accomplishment in any cooperative endeavor. Projects can be made to run smoothly in any type of partnership.

Mars Opposite Saturn (♂☍♄)

Saturn's caution tends to oppose or oppress the energy and initiative of Mars. Mars in time becomes rebellious and defiant toward Saturn. Mars' enterprise, daring, and impetuosity can prove disturbing to the cautious, prudent, "play safe" instincts in Saturn. However, in some causes, the caution of Saturn can be a good balance for the headstrong tendency of Mars. The combination can work out well where there are many good aspects in the comparison, indicating by other combinations that the two individuals can cooperate with each other. But if there are a majority of testing aspects, this Saturn-Mars opposition merely adds another discord to the picture.

Mars Square Saturn (♂□♄)

Saturn frustrates Mars, making the latter impatient, angry, and resistant. Mars irritates and unsettles the constructive ideas and efforts of Saturn and the security feelings of Saturn. This aspect treats many problems of adjustment. The Saturn individual will be critical of Mars' ambition and enterprise. At times the caution, prudence, and conservative instinct of Saturn can prevent Mars from reckless ventures or losses, though Mars may not appreciate this until long afterward. In marriage it is best if the woman's Saturn aspects the man's Mars rather than vice versa. Much depends upon other aspects if this can or cannot be resolved by the individuals. The aspect intensifies any friction or antagonism indicated by other frictional aspects.

Mars Conjunct Uranus (♂☌♅)

This aspect brings out the aggressive and independent spirit in each, which can cause considerable friction unless the ambitions coincide. It will be difficult for two individuals to achieve constant harmony and to cooperate where this aspect occurs. One will irritate the other sooner or later, though to what degree depends on other aspects. If the individuals happen to be engaged in scientific, inventive, or mechanical activities, the aspect can prove stimulating, but as a rule this aspect brings out the more aggressive and rebellious side in the natures. Neither can depend fully on the other, and if the association is close, as in marriage, parent-child or other family bonds, it can affect the nervous system of one or both individuals since the reaction is emotional. In romance there would be periodic emotional upsets and uncertainties. In marriage there is apt to be much turmoil. It does not promote feelings of security with or dependability on each other. The aspect is not conducive to endurability in any close association unless there are a large number of harmonious aspects and the individuals are highly developed in a spiritual sense or have achieved self-mastery of their emotions and tempers.

Mars Sextile or Trine Uranus (♂✶♅, ♂△♅)

These aspects stimulate originality, creative ability, inventiveness, independence, enterprise, and sense of adventure in a productive and progressive way. The individuals encourage confidence and initiative in each other. They will benefit each other through the association.

Mars Opposite or Square Uranus (♂☍♅, ♂□♅)

Here there will be a conflict of individual wills. It is difficult for the individuals to cooperate fully. Mars resents the independence and altruistic or impersonal side of Uranus. Mars cannot depend on Uranus in all situations. The individuals have an irritating effect on each other which in time can affect the nervous system in either or both. Unless individuals are very tolerant and patient with each other, these aspects are unfortunate for marriage. Marriage could end in separation or divorce, especially if the individuals try to mix marriage with business partnership. The association may have a chance if the individuals are occasionally or periodically separated.

Mars Conjunct Neptune (♂♂Ψ)

Whether this aspect is favorable depends on other aspects in the comparison. Mars excites the emotional quality in Neptune. Neptune can inspire Mars and help Mars to simulate the desire nature. Neptune encourages Mars to broaden the scope of ambitions and achievements. For any joint artistic, dramatic or musical interests, this aspect has creative value. In adverse charts Mars will confuse Neptune and over-stimulate the imagination; Neptune will sap the courage of Mars. There is much wasted emotion and effort. Neptune may prove deceptive or evasive to Mars in some way. In marriage the aspect is not very good, especially if the man's Mars is on the woman's Neptune. Mars emits anxiety and fears. If the Neptune individual procrastinates the Mars influence will irritate, though it will also stimulate more action. In an association of any duration the Neptune influence will triumph, wearing down much of the Mars vitality and initiative. This is a bad aspect if one or both tend to habitual self-indulgence, such as in alcohol.

Mars Sextile or Trine Neptune (♂⚹Ψ, ♂△Ψ)

The influence of Neptune in combination with any planet is more subtle and emotional than objective. Here the initiative of Mars and the idealism, sacrificial tendency, and psychic perception of Neptune can combine for a creative effect. Neptune can inspire Mars or soothe the latter when feelings ate ruffled. Mars can help Neptune fight inertia or procrastination. The combination can be especially effective if there is a mutual interest in psychic phenomena, mysticism, astrology or scientific, industrial or political research.

Mars Opposite or Square Neptune (♂☍Ψ, ♂□Ψ)

These aspects cause emotional disturbances in one or both individuals. Mars is abrupt and impatient; Neptune is elusive or deceptive in reaction to Mars' aggressiveness. The Mars directness-Neptune detachment creates irritation or misunderstanding rather than harmony in these combinations. If Neptune is high excitable, Mars can upset the poise, even the health, of the Neptune individual. The aspect also endangers waste, extravagance, or dissipation. Horoscopes with this combination must be carefully analyzed for any possible demoralizing influence.

Mars Sextile or Trine Pluto (♂✶♀, ♂△♀)

These aspects encourage mutual interests and prospects for large-scale operations undertaken together. They are good if individuals are interested in research, engineering, mechanics, industry, labor, politics or civic affairs. The individuals can strengthen each other's will power. Very good in business associations, as they assist progress.

Mars Conjunct, Opposite or Square Pluto (♂♂♀, ♂♂♀, ♂□♀)

There is a conflict of wills and interference with each other. Resistance is made to any show of authority in either. Minor irritations are augured if charts are dominantly harmonious. If charts are dominantly discordant, there can be violent reactions to each other. Each resists any show of "bossiness" in the other. They can hinder each other's efforts and also be vindictive toward each other. In marriage the aspect denotes problems of sexual adjustment, and the conjunction can induce sexual perversions if either party is inclined that way.

Jupiter

For Jupiter's aspects to Sun, Moon, Mercury, Venus, and Mars see pages 53, 61, 67, 70, 71, and 75.

Jupiter Conjunct, Sextile, or Trine Jupiter (♃♂♃, ♃✶♃, ♃△♃)

These aspects denote similarity, if not complete agreement, in ideals, ethics, aspirations, and religious or spiritual concepts. The individuals will inspire much good in each other and will encourage optimism, self-confidence, and humor, and will benefit each other or protect each other in many ways. There is much companionship, mutual interests, and mutual appreciation. They usually look for each other's good qualities and appreciate them. Any of these three is a good aspect to find in marriage or family comparison. Individuals are tolerant, considerate and forgiving toward each other.

Jupiter Opposite or Square Jupiter (♃♂♃, ♃□♃)

There may be differences in aspirations, religious ideas, ideals, moral sentiments, ethics, and fundamental spiritual leanings in the individuals. Ideas of fair play and justice may differ. In the square a difference of religious beliefs can cause misunderstandings, especially if either of the individuals inclines toward the fanatical. Differences in concept regarding ethical procedures in business or other affairs also can create problems of adjustment. The opposition and square of Jupiter to Jupiter are not harmfully adverse unless the comparison chart is extremely discordant. Then it merely adds emphasis to the other conflicts.

Jupiter Conjunct, Sextile, or Trine Saturn (♃☌♄, ♃⚹♄, ♃△♄)

These are favorable aspects for most relationships and particularly for business. The prudence and conservatism of Saturn blends well with the expansion, promotional ability, and optimism of Jupiter to create good administrative policies. The two individuals can advise each other well and can unite their efforts effectively. In the conjunction, the Saturn individual will need to guard against being too critical or cautious or he will dampen the enthusiasm that is natural to Jupiter. If the Jupiter person tends to be overconfident or reckless, this Saturn influence is an advantage, not a detriment.

Jupiter Opposite or Square Saturn (♃☍♄, ♃□♄)

Saturn delays, resists, and puts obstacles in the path of Jupiter's aspirations. There can be disagreement on financial or business procedures where one of these aspects occurs. Saturn criticizes, limits, or places too much burden or responsibility on Jupiter. The Jupiter expansiveness feels confined and frustrated. The Jupiter individual may have to relinquish many aspirations, or even opportunities, in any close association that includes one of these aspects. Saturn can be or will seem unjust at times and can be selfish, demanding, and even undermine the confidence of Jupiter. If the Jupiter individual has strong spiritual beliefs and faith, the experiences incurred with the Saturn individual will test him. In some causes, the Saturn testing will strengthen Jupiter's faith, but only after a mighty inward struggle.

Jupiter Conjunct, Sextile, or Trine Uranus (♃☌♅, ♃⚹♅, ♃△♅)

Humanitarian qualities of personality are brought out in both individuals where one of these aspects occurs. They will respect each other's need for freedom and individuality of expression. They can encourage the development in each other of talents and self-expression, as well as ideals and altruistic views. They inspire each other in many ways. There is much stimulus of ideas, ideals, and creative objectives; also many mutual recreational enjoyments. The conjunction needs control, however, as there is a tendency to excite overconfidence, or any recklessness or gambling tendencies lurking in either personality.

Jupiter Opposite or Square Uranus (♃☍♅, ♃△♅)

These aspects tend to excite radical views and differences in social or religious ideas. They stimulate considerable extravagance, recklessness, and resistance to responsibility in one or both individuals. In the square the aspirations and ideals of Jupiter will conflict with the personal attitudes and individualistic ideas of Uranus. Uranus will seem rebellious, inconsistent, or unstable to Jupiter. Uranus will interrupt plans of Jupiter and try his patience.

Jupiter Conjunct, Sextile, or Trine Neptune (♃☌♆, ♃⚹♆, ♃△♆)

There is encouragement of idealism, spiritual or religious interests, and charitable instincts in each other. There is often a strong psychic tie. Both planets are expansive and so can encourage efforts toward realization of material ambitions, too. In the case of business associates, the aspect in propitious for the accumulation of wealth if the charts are harmonious and show good endurability. The conjunction is a good aspect if found in horoscopes of spiritually developed or self-disciplined individuals, but not so good if individuals are weak and given to dissolute habits. In such cases, it is apt to encourage self-indulgence.

Jupiter Opposite or Square Neptune (♃☍♆, ♃△♆)

There is a tendency to bring out impractical qualities or irresponsible tendencies in one, if not both, individuals. The Neptune individual may be tempted to cheat or deceive Jupiter. Where one of these aspects occurs, the confidence of Jupiter in the Neptune individual will be tested in some way. Neptune will often prove elusive, hard to pin down, thus making Jupiter fret, for he prefers to trust rather than to doubt another. This aspect is to be avoided in business or marriage unless there are many good aspects to promise mutual confidence. Where charts indicate a majority of mutually beneficial qualities, this Jupiter-Neptune combination might indicate merely minor irritations due to differences in religious or spiritual ideals.

Jupiter Sextile or Trine Pluto (♃⚹♇, ♃△♇)

Encourages philanthropic interests and efforts, character improvements, and spiritual evolvement in the individuals. Also stimulates increase and abundance in material ways. Encourages large-scale interests and enlarging the field of expression and general progress.

Jupiter Opposite or Square Pluto (♃☍♇, ♃□♇)

Frustrating, conflicting aspirations and ideals can create misunderstanding or make cooperation difficult. These are spiritually testing, especially to the Jupiter individual.

Jupiter Conjunct Pluto (♃☌♇)

This aspect is variable as it can be either favorable or unfavorable depending on other combinations in the comparison. The Pluto individual can be possessive and domineering, but Jupiter will inspire and encourage Pluto as a rule. The aspect benefits Pluto more than Jupiter. It sometimes indicates financial success in business, marriage, or political partnerships.

Saturn

For Saturn with Sun, Moon, Mercury, Venus, Mars, and Jupiter see pages 54, 55, 61-63, 67, 68, 71, 72, 75-77, 80.

Saturn Conjunct Saturn (♄☌♄)

There will be a similarity of attitude in regard to security and ambitions. Individuals will understand each other's security urges. They may have similar problems, responsibilities, and limitations. In harmonious charts this aspect aids constructive efforts toward a common goal. However, they are likely to experience similar problems also, and their attitude toward duty or responsibility being similar, it can swing their approach to their shared problems too much one way, thus handicapping their progress together. The reaction on each other will increase any tendency in to fear, worry, or lack of self-confidence. Unless there are many aspects stimulating hope, optimism, and activity to balance this one, they could have a devitalizing effect on each other.

Saturn Sextile or Trine Saturn (♄⚹♄, ♄△♄)

The two can cooperate in anything involving work or responsibility or where problems of security are being worked out. This can be a very good aspect in marriage, business, or any type of partnership. A similar attitude toward responsibility helps them to agree and cooperate in meeting obligations. Usually they have a common goal.

Saturn Opposite or Square Saturn (♄☍♄, ♄△♄)

There is a conflict in the attitude toward and handling of responsibility and security. Unless very strong aspects offset this one, they can discourage, limit, or frustrate each other, or one of the individuals will affect the other negatively. Sometimes this leads to mutual distrust. It could even affect the health of one or both. These aspects are discouraging, devitalizing, and create serious problems of adjustment. In marriage each may have burdens, problems, or obligations which handicap the harmony unity, financial security, and happiness of the union. Family or parental difficulties may be a stumbling block. If individuals incur heavy debts after marriage it increases worry and obstructs success and economic prosperity.

Saturn Conjunct Uranus (♄☌♅)

Saturn caution and deliberation can help Uranus ingenuity find practical and constructive channels. The aspirational traits of Uranus can stimulate the material ambitions of Saturn. The vision of Uranus can prevent Saturn anxiety from turning into apprehension or fear. Uranus makes Saturn more progressive and more adaptable to change. Saturn prudence and desire to consolidate keeps the Uranian urge for independence from becoming mere erratic instability or irresponsibility.

The old and the new which Saturn and Uranus symbolize can combine to good advantage. But Saturn must be flexible and Uranus must accept responsibility if this aspect is to work for mutual benefit. The combination can be good in various types of business partnerships where creative ability, invention, or any typical Saturn or Uranus interests are involved. In marriage much patience will be needed. Freedom (Uranus) and bondage (Saturn) are contradictory instincts which can unite only when there is complete understanding, real love, and respect.

Saturn Sextile or Trine Uranus (♄✶♅, ♄△♅)

These aspects aid the industry and progressiveness of both individuals. New ideas (Uranus) can unite with experience and caution (Saturn) for cooperative efforts toward a constructive goal.

Saturn Opposite or Square Uranus (♄☍♅, ♄□♅)

Uranus will stimulate Saturn but can have a disorganizing effect upon the plans and efforts of the latter. Saturn wants solidarity but Uranus wants change. To Saturn, Uranus seems undependable, unstable, and erratic in these aspects, and Saturn's slowness or caution will irk Uranus. These are antagonistic aspects for most associations. The square causes the most serious friction, arousing many irritations and frustrations; one individual will create problems of adjustment for the other. Saturn will delay progress of Uranus or restrict his freedom to operate in his own sphere of expression. Uranus will often rebel against the restrictions of Saturn. But the problems such individuals encounter together provide opportunity for spiritual evolvement in both.

Saturn Conjunct Neptune (♄☌♆)

Saturn disciplines Neptune, and restrains the emotions and imagination of Neptune. Neptune can raise Saturn's ambitions to a more spiritual level. This is a harmless combination in most cases, but neither is it especially beneficial. In some cases it creates doubt of each other, misunderstanding, and deception. It is doubtful for associations involving financial transactions. Saturn forces responsibility on Neptune which they the latter will not appreciate.

Saturn Sextile or Trine Neptune (♄✶♆, ♄△♆)

Neptune can be an inspiration to Saturn. Saturn can stabilize Neptune. This is a harmonious aspect but not a very important one.

Saturn Opposite or Square Neptune (♄☍♆, ♄□♆)

Neptune will be aloof or evasive, Saturn restricting and limiting. These aspects tend to breed misunderstanding and deception on the part of one or both. Saturn will seem selfish and domineering to Neptune.

Neptune will seem ineffectual and a daydreamer to Saturn. Neptune would have to make the most concessions to ensure harmony in an association. It is unfavorable for financial dealings between persons, or for political or governmental associations.

Saturn Sextile or Trine Pluto (♄⚹♇, ♄△♇)

These aspects aid joint planning and uniting efforts for large-scale enterprises. They stimulate the ability to make good use of experience. The aspects are good for individuals engaged in research, experimentation, industry, government, politics, banking, building, mining, discovery and development of natural resources, or in law enforcement. It is not very important in horoscopes of marriage partners or persons whose attachment is mainly emotional.

Saturn Conjunct, Opposite or Square Pluto (♄☌♇, ♄☍♇, ♄□♇)

Pluto is the transformer or reformer and challenges the Saturn attitude toward his own responsibilities of life. If the majority of aspects in the comparison are harmonious, an unfavorable Saturn-Pluto combination will be mildly testing. If there are many adverse aspects, such a combination indicates mutual resentment, hateful attitudes, and desire to harm each other. An especially difficult combination when found in charts of a parent-child relationship.

Uranus

For Uranus aspects to Sun, Moon, Mercury, Venus, Mars, Jupiter, and Saturn see pages 55, 56, 63, 64, 68, 72, 77, 78, 80, 81, 82, and 83.

Uranus Conjunct Uranus (♅☌♅)

Uranus in the same sign means that the individuals are contemporaries - born within seven years of each other, if not the same year; or they could be 84 years apart. In the case of the 84-year difference it is doubtful if the individuals would have much, if any, effect upon each other. At best, Uranus in the same sign would indicate merely mutual appreciation. The older individual would understand many of the younger's urges for self-expression and independence. Individuals who are contemporaries would react in a similar way to new inventions, developments in science, mechanics, education, government changes or the like. They may have similar interests in metaphysics or the unique or unusual.

Uranus Sextile or Trine Uranus (♅⚹♅, ♅△♅)

Agreement along lines of science, new inventions, changes to be made affecting society in general is indicated. The individuals understand each other's ideals. There may be numerous mutual interests, especially along metaphysical or inventive or creative lines.

Uranus Square Uranus (♅□♅)

There is a sixteen to twenty-one year age difference with the square. This is to be found often in horoscopes of parents and children. It may simply indicate a different point of view in matters regarding society due to the trend of the times. It is not apt to cause friction until the younger person reaches a more adult age beginning at about age eighteen or nineteen.

Uranus Opposite Uranus (♅☍♅)

There is a thirty-seven to forty-two year age difference. This aspect, like the square, simply indicates a different viewpoint of life due to trends of the times and past experience of the older person. An older person who has retained his understanding of youth and has patience with youth can bridge the gap of age, and thus, this aspect will not be of much significance. But if the horoscopes are very antagonistic, both the opposition and square of Uranus to Uranus will increase the hostility and may cause estrangements, and the younger is sure to revolt against the older.

Uranus Conjunct, Sextile, or Trine Neptune (♅☌♆, ♅⚹♆, ♅△♆)

Mutual interests of an occult, mystic, or psychic nature are likely to be found in individuals having one of these combinations in the comparison chart. There may be similarity of social or political views. These aspects are favorable, but not especially important in themselves. They add weight to other harmonious interchart aspects.

The conjunction can be unfavorable in some cases, since it will encourage irresponsibility in persons who are inclined to evade responsibility.

Uranus Opposite or Square Neptune (♅☍♆, ♅□♆)

There may be differences in social or political views, but this depends on other aspects. Sometimes differences in aspirations or ideals. These aspects will magnify other discords found in comparisons; otherwise they are not important in themselves.

Uranus Sextile or Trine Pluto (♅□♇, ♅△♇)

Mutually encouraging for versatility of self-expression or for spiritual unfoldment in either or both individuals.

Uranus Opposite or Square Pluto (♅☍♇, ♅□♇)

Indicates confusions and conflict of spiritual goals. The testings are mostly on the spiritual level here. Importance of aspects depends on other aspects in the chart.

Uranus Conjunct Pluto (♅☌♇)

This is variable, either favorable or unfavorable, depending on the comparison as a whole. The individuals will either resist each other or will unite their interests and efforts effectively.

Neptune

For Neptune aspects to Sun, Moon, Mercury Venus, Mars, Jupiter, Saturn, and Uranus see pages 56, 57, 64, 68, 69, 72, 73, 78, 81, 83, 84, and 85.

Neptune Conjunct or Sextile Neptune (♆☌♆, ♆⚹♆)

These aspects indicate sympathy of ideals. Mutual interests, such as music, drama, poetry, mysticism or psychic phenomena, religion, or politics increase any liking the individuals have for each other. Alas, too, it stimulates any mutual tendency toward dissipation or escape habits.

It requires thirty-seven years for Neptune to square itself, fifty-three years for the trine and seventy-nine years for the opposition. Changing times indicate changing conditions, different viewpoints in individuals. These aspects have little significance other than that of the natural differences of age and experience.

Neptune with Pluto

Similar to Uranus-Pluto combinations.

Pluto

For Pluto aspects to other planets see pages 57, 58, 64, 65, 69, 73, 74, 79, 81, 82, 84, 85, and 86.

Pluto Conjunct Pluto (♇☌♇)

Pluto in the same sign simply indicates that the individuals live through periods of similar "world" conditions, and their ideas and viewpoints will be conditioned in similar directions unless the individuals have achieved an unusual degree of spiritual freedom, self-dependence and ability to think for themselves. This aspect is not very important in describing the reaction of personality on personality.

Pluto is the vagrant of the Zodiac. Its path around the Sun is irregular. At one point it crosses inside the orbit of Neptune. Its cycle through a sign is erratic. It was thirty years in Gemini, twenty-five years in Cancer, and only nineteen years in Leo. For this reason it is impossible to say at what approximate ages the sextile or square would be formed. To form a trine would take 100 years or more. It would be rarely encountered in comparing horoscopes. The aspects are not of importance as far as describing reaction of personality traits is concerned.

Appendix

Symbols of the Signs

Aries—♈   Libra—♎
Taurus—♉   Scorpio—♏
Gemini—♊   Sagittarius—♐
Cancer—♋   Capricorn—♑
Leo—♌   Aquarius—♒
Virgo—♍   Pisces—♓

Symbols of the Sun, Moon and Planets

Sun—☉   Saturn—♄
Moon—☽   Uranus—♅
Mercury—☿   Neptune—♆
Venus—♀   Pluto—♇
Mars—♂   Moon's North Node—☊
Jupiter—♃   Moon's South Node—☋

Aspects

Conjunction (☌): Planets in the same sign, or within 10 degrees of each other.

Opposition (☍): Planets in opposite signs, or within 170 to 190 degrees of each other.

Square (□): Planets three signs apart, or within 80 to 100 degrees of each other.

Sextile (✳): Planets two signs apart, or within 50 to 70 degrees of each other.

Trine (△): Planets four signs apart, or within 110 to 130 degrees of each other.